ANOTHER TIME, ANOTHER PLACE

ANOTHER TIME, ANOTHER PLACE

The True Story of a Teenage Mother in the '50s

Rose Handleigh-Adams

Book Guild Publishing

Sussex, England

First published in Great Britain in 2013 by
The Book Guild Ltd
Pavilion View
19 New Road
Brighton, BN1 1UF

Typesetting in Garamond by
YHT Ltd, London

Printed and bound in Great Britain by
CPI Group (UK) Ltd, Croydon, CR0 4YY

A catalogue record for this book is available from
The British Library.

ISBN 978 1 84624 842 9

Acknowledgements

To my late husband, Charles Adams, who never did get to read this book.
To my dearest friend, Brenda Jackman, who always believed in me and was always there for me.
To the late Stanley Kirby, who was a very dear friend of my family.
To Bruce Bellringer who gave me the encouragement to write my story.
To my dear friend, Leslie Allport, for giving me the encouragement to go ahead and have this story published.

Chapter 1

The August storm lit up the sky in a jagged display of energy, flashing lights brightening the room for a few seconds before a loud boom shook the very foundations of the building. Only it was not an electric thunder storm that Helen could hear; it was something far more sinister. She gave a cry as a pain shot through her body again; they were coming every few minutes now and each one greater than the one before. The sound of the sirens grew even more urgent and the beams of light circled the ward as the spotlights searched the night sky for the German Luftwaffe's bombers as they droned across London to drop their deadly load. Helen's cry was lost; drowned out by the new sound of Spitfires as they skimmed the sky ready to stop the enemy aircraft in their tracks. They were now almost overhead. A plane was targeted and Helen could hear the whirl as it spiralled towards the ground. She cried out 'God help us all' before another contraction shook her body. Beads of perspiration trickled down her face. The room lit up again – another strike – followed by an explosion and Helen gave a cry and an almighty push and I was born into this hostile world. The year was 1940, and the place Central Middlesex Hospital, Park Royal, London, in the centre of the industrial area that Germany was trying to raze to the ground during the Battle of Britain in the Second World War. Mum trembled as she held me close, her first-born, not knowing what sort of future, if any, we would have. Exhausted, tears filled her eyes with joy and sorrow.

My father, Norman, had come from Gateshead in County Durham to London in 1939, just as the Second World War started, to work in the Lancaster, Dynamo and Crypto, a metal machine making factory. The factory was known locally as 'The Crypto'. Dad met my mother Helen, who was also working there, and it seemed they hit it off straight away, as I arrived six months after they were hastily married in a small church in Willesden.

The Blitz continued. Bombs were dropping every night and day. Many houses and factories were taking direct hits and thousands of people lost their lives and many others were left with only craters and rubble where their homes had once stood.

Dad joined the Home Guard, which was a part-time civilian army formed to protect the home front. The Home Guard was the first citizens' army since Napoleon threatened invasion in the nineteenth century and it was considered to play an important role in the war-torn towns, cities and around the coast of Britain.

The landscape of London was forever changing due to the night-time raids, but Mum and Dad did not want to go into the bomb shelters at night as Mum had said that none of Hitler's bombs was going to drive them out of their home, so instead we would cuddle up on a mattress under the table with chicken wire around it. I don't suppose this would have saved us if the house in Harlesden had taken a direct hit. Despite the war, everyday life had to go on as best it could. Shops and factories, if they had not been destroyed, tried to function as normally as possible. There was rationing and a shortage of food and clothing. Long queues of people would be waiting outside the shops to buy whatever food was available. Dried egg powder for breakfast or lunchtime, and bags of bones from the butchers would give vegetable stew a lovely flavour. Many people grew vegetables and had apple and pear trees in their gardens or allotments. Rhubarb was very popular but cooked with little or no sugar as sugar was on ration.

When I was about ten months old Mum was waiting in a queue inside a baker's shop – I was left outside in the pram – when the noise of the air-raid warning sounded and enemy aircraft could be heard. I was screaming as the noise was deafening and people were running for cover. Mum came rushing out from the shop, snatched me from the pram, rushed back inside and dropped to the floor with her body protecting me. The bomb landed, with a great loud, ear-splitting bang nearby and the shop window shattered, sending glass crashing to the floor. Mum was just thankful the bomb had not dropped onto the shop. Although Mum was worried by the bombing, she did not want me to be parted from her and evacuated to live with strangers as I was so young.

One day I was playing on the floor next to the grate in the living room. I dropped a penny and a spoon down a hole I had been digging at, and I then burst into tears. Mum picked me up and rocking me from side to side asked Dad to see if he could climb down through a gap at the back of the coal cellar beneath the stairs to retrieve whatever I had dropped down there. Dad climbed through the gap at the back of the cupboard and jumped down with his torch at the ready. He made his way to below the hole in the grate and playfully shone his torch upwards, which made me giggle. Next thing was Dad scrambling back through the hole as if the devil himself was after him. Black-faced and his blue eyes wide open behind his brown-framed glasses, he blurted out to Mum that there was a skeleton in the cellar.

'Don't be daft, Norman. Course there isn't, Stop messing about!'

3

'I'm telling you, Nell,' replied Dad, excitedly pointing to the floor, 'there's a skeleton down there.'

Mum looked worried as she rocked me in her arms. 'Is it an animal's skeleton?'

'No, it's definitely a human skeleton.'

'What shall we do about it then, Norman?'

Dad thought for a while as he paced back and forth.

'We'll do nothing,' he eventually said. 'There's a war on and we don't want the police here, do we? We could be chucked out onto the streets by the landlord. No, we'll do nothing and say nothing to anyone, so keep your lips zipped.'

Next day Dad bricked up the back of the cellar, sealing in the macabre discovery. For all I know it is there to this day.

With the war still raging, Mum was eventually persuaded by Dad to send me to Gateshead to stay with my dad's parents.

I was named after my paternal grandmother, Rose, a very small, dark, curly-haired lady who had a warm friendly smile and had a laugh like a gentle melody. Grandma was always busy pottering about doing something or other, cooking, dusting or tidying up. She would be up about five o' clock in the morning to go down the iron steps at the back of the house to empty the white chamber pots into the outside toilet, then she would clean the black stove, light the fire with sticks of wood and newspaper before putting the coal on the flickering flames. Next she'd make the upstairs flat spick and span before doing breakfast and going out shopping. My grandfather looked an older version of my father; light-brown hair parted at the side and long strands brushed over the balding head, he had the same clear blue eyes behind brown-framed glasses. He was a kindly jovial man who had a lovely smile and a ready laugh between puffing on his pipe. He was not a well man a lot of the time as he had been affected by poison gas during the First World War. I was about three years old when I went to stay with them in the upper-floor flat in a terraced house at the top of a very steep hill. On a heavy rainy day, I would watch the water flowing down the road like a river, and during the winter, on icy days, no one attempted to venture down the road at the front but would go out to the back alley and steady themselves on the cobbles and walls as they made their way downhill. The front doors of the houses all opened up onto the pavement, not that people closed their doors during the day, as the doors were open for anyone to call in for a cup of tea and a chat. The houses had two doors each, one for the downstairs flat and one for the upstairs. I would love it when my Uncle John, my dad's brother, came to visit with his wife, Aunty Betty. I don't remember having any toys to play with so I enjoyed playing with their daughter, Mary, who was a day older than me; she had a ragdoll that she would let me hold and play with. Sometimes Uncle Ray, another of Dad's brothers, would visit and the grown-up chat was always about what was happening in the war and the latest bombing raids on London and wondering whether Dad and my mother had survived. Sometimes we could hear bombs dropping on Newcastle.

I slept in a large room that was very cold and the white cotton sheets were freezing until they were warmed up by my body heat. I covered my ears with the blankets to keep them warm, but stepping onto the linoleum floor when getting out of a warm bed in the morning was like walking on a sheet of ice. The toilet was outside at the back of the house, next to the gate leading into the alleyway. We had to go down iron steps to reach the old brick shed that housed it. There were no toilet rolls, just squares of newspaper stuck onto a nail. The chain was a length of string and the seat was a wooden split bench. The wind and cold would blow under the wooden door so much that it was too uncomfortable to sit there for very long. Grandma would put the large white china potties under each of the beds at night.

We always had plenty of food even though a war was on.

There were homemade fruit pies and fish-paste sandwiches and tea made with sterilized milk. The black-bottomed kettle was always at the ready on the hob to make tea in the brown china teapot. Granddad would sit by the black Aga, which Grandma would have cleaned spotless with black lead polish after she had done her cooking in the oven. Granddad would choose one of his many pipes that were kept on the high mantelpiece, then spent time cleaning and poking the tobacco into the bowl before lighting and smoking it, poking and lighting it again, whilst listening to the radio before he would take a nap. He usually gave me a few furry pipe cleaners for me to play with and I would twist and curl them into shapes of little people or animals. It was comforting to me to smell the tobacco and cooking – it made me feel happy and so much a part of this family. Life was so normal and everyone went about their business as if the war wasn't on. Granddad was a carpenter by trade and one day he made me a small chest-of-drawers toy money box. It was really a work of art and the wood shone with polish. I would open one of the two drawers at the top, put a penny in, close it and the penny would drop inside.

Sometimes Uncle Jimmy, Uncle John and Uncle Ray would visit and the room would be full of smoke as they puffed away. They were so jolly and laughingly they would pick me up and swing me in the air and tickle me in fun. When I contracted measles my grandmother took good care of me and when I felt better, but still smothered in spots, she took me for a walk to meet up with other children so they could catch it and get it out the way. Once I wet the bed and Grandma shamed me by telling everybody she met what I had done and I never ever dared to wet the bed again.

The whole country celebrated when the news came through on the wireless in the May of 1945 that Hitler was dead and Germany had surrendered. People were dancing in the streets and kissing and hugging each other, but it was not until the July that my father came to take me home. I could hardly remember my dad and it was such a wrench to leave my grandma and granddad that I cried so loud the whole of the street must have heard me. Dad and I travelled by tram to the rail station in Newcastle, to catch the green-and-black Flying Scotsman to King's Cross. I looked on in awe as the giant monster with wheels puffed out bellows of smoke from the chimney in preparation for the journey. When the brakes were tested, the noise was ear-splitting and we couldn't hear ourselves speak, yet it was so exciting for a little girl like me to see this wonderful train. Dad lifted me up to see the train driver and his fireman, shovelling the coal into the furnace. We then got into the third-class carriage and found a seat to settle down into for the long seven- or eight-hour journey. It did not take me long to fall asleep to the sound of clicketty-clicketty-click of the wheels on the tracks.

When we arrived in London it was dark and Dad, who was only about 5 feet 3 inches but quite muscular, carried me, as well as the cases, for a while before we got onto the bus going to Harlesden. I was almost asleep as Dad took my hand to steady me over the rubble and bricks as we walked past the bombed-out buildings and finally arrived at the road we lived in. I was so tired and weary after the long journey and it was a relief when we finally arrived at the Victorian terraced house, 17 St John's Avenue. Dad put the key in the lock and opened the door with one hand whilst holding me up with the other. He wore a grey trilby hat on his balding head, and he straightened it before we went in. It was eerily quiet and dark as we walked along the passageway and down the two steps leading to a door at the back of the house. I had no idea how my life would change once I had passed through that door.

Chapter 2

Dad ushered me into a small room that was filled with a lot of people. My mother, whom I hardly recognized at first, said, 'Hello, Rosie.' She gave Dad a peck on the cheek, whilst rocking a screaming baby in her arms.

I was so overwhelmed by these strangers that I hid behind my father's jacket. A thin woman, who was wearing a scarf tied in a turban over her curlers, stood holding a small boy by the hand. In her other hand she had a cigarette which she puffed on, sending a ring of smoke into the already-smoky room, I learnt later that she was my mother's sister, Ann. A man, wearing a shirt and braces, was standing beside Aunty Ann; this was her husband, Len. Three young children were sitting on the floor silently staring at me. My grandfather, 'Pop', was sitting hunched up on a coal box by the grate. A couple of old shoes were burning on the fire and he was almost coughing his heart out.

I clung to my father's hand. 'Daddy,' I whispered, 'who are all these people and who are all these kids?'

Dad turned to my mother. 'She's tired, Nell. She will want to sleep, and it's been a long journey.'

Mum handed the screaming baby to Aunty Ann then took my hand, 'Come on, Rosie, I'll take you to your bed. Do you want a cup of tea or a piece of bread first? If you do, I'll bring it in to you.'

'No thank you,' I replied in my Geordie accent. I didn't have the energy to eat or drink anything. Mum took my hand and I was taken back along the blacked-out passageway to the room at the front of the house. Mum helped take off my dress and shoes and socks in the darkened room and then put me into the bed. I fell asleep almost immediately.

Next morning I awoke with a hard kick in my back. It was my brother Norman who was aged about three; he had a snotty nose that he stuck his finger into. He looked bewildered as he stared at me, but said nothing. He stuck his 'green candlestick' back up his nose. Suddenly feeling sick, I jumped out of the bed quickly. The bed was covered with old coats instead of blankets and there was only one sheet to sleep on. I was not used to sharing a bed or having no sheets or proper blankets.

I left Norman and gingerly went along the passageway, down the two steps to a scullery on the left-hand side, where my mother was filling the kettle up at the large square white butler sink. She turned to me. 'Do you want a cup of tea and a slice of bread?' I soon learnt that a cup of tea and a slice of bread would be my main diet from now on.

Mum pointed to a door leading off from the scullery. 'That's the toilet in there.' I went in, surprised that there was a toilet inside the house. There was also a bath which was filled with junk and screwed-up newspapers and rags, and it did not look as if the bath had any connecting pipes to the water taps. I was thinking what a strange house this was, with a toilet indoors and a bath that didn't look as if anyone had ever used it.

I heard a noise coming from the back room. I went to investigate and saw my baby brother, Kenneth, lying on the settee. Tears welled up in my eyes. I hated it here. I wanted to be back with my grandparents in Gateshead. The baby did not have a nappy on, so he was crying and kicking his legs furiously as if he were riding a bike. 'Shut up!' I said. He hesitated for a moment his bottom lip quivered, then he began to cry even louder, so in frustration I pushed him off the settee and he landed with a thud on the floor. He then squealed even more. Mum came rushing in and picked him up and tried to soothe him. 'Hush there... shush, shush. How did you end up down there on the floor, my little boy?' She nursed him until he stopped crying. She never did find out it was me who pushed him off the settee.

After I had eaten a doorstep slice of bread and dripping and tea made with condensed milk, I went along the passageway and heard angry voices coming from upstairs.

'You stupid idiot, get out of my sight!' shouted a woman.

I crouched down and looked through the wooden banisters. A man wearing a shabby coat and trousers sat himself down at the top of the stairs. He was tapping his clothes nervously as if checking his pockets and adjusting the string which held his trousers up. He suddenly noticed me watching him.

I took a quick step back. 'Hello,' he said, grinning and moving his head from side to side as if his collar was itching his neck. 'Who are you?'

'I'm Rose,' I said, 'What do they call you then?'

'I'm George,' he said, picking at his jacket.

The unknown woman shouted again. 'Get your arse moving to the shop right now and this time take the bloody ration book with you, and stop talking to yourself or they'll put you away.'

George shuffled up out of sight then hurried down the stairs and out of the front door, which he slammed with such a force that it was a good job the door had cardboard where the glass had once been or it would have smashed. The woman with the loud voice peered over the banisters to see if George had really been talking to somebody. She saw me and came hurrying down the stairs. She was wearing a ragged coat that had been cut up and stitched into a skirt; she also wore a brown knitted jumper that was out of shape.

'Hello,' she said kindly. 'You're Rosie! You're home... My word, haven't you grown and so pretty, too. Would you like a sweet?' She handed me a green wine gum from her pocket. It was covered in fluff. This woman was my grandmother, Nancy.

She called up the stairs. 'Hey, Billy, come here and say hello to Rosie.' A thin boy about fifteen years old with an almost hunched-up back and wearing grey trousers that looked too short for him and an untidy shirt and reddish pullover came running down the stairs. 'It's your Uncle Billy,' said my grandmother.

I said 'Hello'. Billy did not say anything; he just turned and ran up the stairs again.

It was a few weeks later that Mum asked Billy to take me to school. It was not the nearest school to our house but the one that the three girls next door would be attending. They were a ginger-haired girl named Sylvia and her younger twin sisters, Pauline and Brenda. The twins were about the same age as me. I had said 'Hello' to them the previous day and they had laughed at the funny way I spoke, but they were nice girls and we played ball up against the air-raid shelters that lined one side of the road, until after a while their mother called them indoors. Their mother was a skinny, timid, unfriendly woman; she did not even say 'Hello' to me. I did not know why people who lived here in London were not as nice as the people in Gateshead, where they would have made me welcome and said a kindly word to me.

Billy took me to school that first day. No one ever came to meet me or take me to school again. I soon learnt to remember the thirty-minute walk to and from school, past the bomb sites and dodging the boys throwing bricks at each other, then past a large estate of flats named Curzon

Crescent. It had a bad reputation that sent a shiver of fear down the spines of many children who had to walk past there. It was where the toughest children from large families lived and they would chase and smack you one if you were not quick enough to escape them.

The first day at school I spent in the nursery class and played in the fenced-off garden area. I peeped through a hole in the fence at the children playing in the playground and saw the teacher, a round woman in a tweed suit, blow on her whistle. All the children stopped whatever they were doing. The second whistle blew and they all scampered into rows two across. Then came the third whistle and the children all walked in an orderly fashion into the school.

The following day I joined the children in the playground and when the large-bosomed teacher in the tweed suit blew her whistle, I stopped still, as did the other children, and waited for the next whistle, quite pleased with myself that I knew what to do. The teacher took one look at me and came striding over.

'You!' she bellowed, pointing her finger into my face. A shiver went down my spine. 'Take that stupid grin off your face!'

I was not aware that I had a grin on my face but nevertheless I tried to keep my face straight.

'I said take that grin off your face!' I could see the hair up her flaring nostrils and felt her spit on my face. I stood as stiff as a poker with my hands at my side. She blew the whistle again but held on to me. 'Not you – you stay where you are.'

The children all walked quietly into the school. The teacher dragged me by the scruff of the neck, through the hall and into her classroom. I stood petrified, facing the class of terrified children who were now standing beside their desks. I felt the teacher's fingers digging into my arm as she held me firmly.

The tweed woman spoke in a low voice: 'Be seated,

everybody.' There was a scraping of chairs as they all sat down. 'Now, class, listen to what I say. When I say, do not do something, I mean it. Do you all understand that?'

'Yes, Miss,' they all replied.

'Well, I am glad about that.' Her other hand grabbed my hair and she shook me violently. Shocked, I winced and struggled. She held me firmly. 'This good-for-nothing does not seem to understand what I say, and for that she will be punished as a lesson to you all.'

She pulled the chair out from under her wooden desk, sat down and put me across her knee. She whacked me over and over again and I was screaming for her to let go of me. When she had finished and she felt that justice had been done, she pointed to the door for me to go. I ran sobbing from the classroom, unable to catch my breath.

This was my introduction to school life and I had now learnt of the violence that grown-ups could inflict upon children and no one even cared about it. Surely, I thought, it could not get any worse than this. But of course it did.

Chapter 3

The Second World War may have ended but the wars at 17 St John's Avenue carried on. If it was not between my father and grandmother, or my father and mother, it was between the neighbours and our family, especially my nan – she hated and distrusted everybody.

My brother David was born in January 1946 at home. I did not know Mum was going to have another baby; he was just there one morning when I went in to see Mum in the bedroom. He was asleep in a drawer, which had been taken out from the bottom of the wardrobe and made into a bed for him.

Later on in 1946 there were going to be street parties to celebrate the end of the war. The people in our road began to club money together every week for the event. One brave lady came to our front door to ask us to contribute. Unluckily for her, my grandmother answered the door and told the poor woman to 'Sling your hook and bugger off our doorstep.' The woman could not get away quick enough. On the day of the party, it started to rain so the neighbours decided to move the event to the church hall. As they were moving the tables, my mum was coming down the road. Mum had previously complained to Aunty Ann and Dad that we children had not been asked to attend the party. Anyway, one of the women gingerly came up to my mum and said, 'Would your children like to come to the party – there would be no charge.' They obviously felt sorry for us being the only children in the road not to be there. Mum replied that we hadn't been asked before so why ask now? It was then that the woman told her what my grandmother had said. Mum was not very happy about this and she agreed to let us go.

My brother Norman and I went to the church hall and as we walked in all eyes were on us. We were directed to our seats and were given a paper plate and cup. A prayer was said by the vicar, thanking the Lord for the end of the war and for the food set before us. A large plate of sandwiches was put on the table and the children dived in. I took a sandwich and opened it to see what was inside – it was fish paste and mustard and cress. As I had never had mustard and cress before, I thought the little black seeds were poison and had been put into the sandwiches by the other kids as we had not paid to go to the party. Even though I wanted to eat the sandwiches I would not. Norman had no such misgivings, he tucked in as if he had not eaten for weeks. I thought he was going to die at any moment, but he was quite happy. Afterwards it was Musical Chairs. The vicar's wife had her back to us all and lifted the arm of the 78 rpm record on the old gramophone and we rushed to get a chair to sit on. The other children took great delight in pushing and thumping Norman and me as hard as they could and they were whispering and laughing at us. I took objection to this, and even though some of the children were much bigger than me I pushed them back with all my might, knocking them over, then I jumped on top of one of them and there was a free-for-all. When the kids ended up crying, the women came rushing to pick them up off the floor, Norman and I were asked to leave.

I did not see a great deal of my father for a while as he had started to work early in the morning and finish late at night. He joined the hundreds of other workers on their bikes going to the factories in the Park Royal area of London. Friday nights Dad went straight to the Crown Hill Working Men's Club. Dad never got drunk, as he could hold his drink, but he often got very merry and he'd be singing with the other drinkers on their way home. My grandmother would shout down the stairs for Dad to shut his noise up, and then he would throw insults back up the stairs to her. Dad always referred to her as 'the Old Girl' and the language was very colourful with swear words I did not understand but knew that they must be bad. Dad would then go and start shouting at my mother. This seemed to be the normal routine and we kids got use to it. Grandfather, whom we referred to as Pop, did not get involved as he was a timid man who suffered with chest problems; he was always coughing and wheezing and that would sap his energy. Pop use to go out with a hand barrow sometimes to collect rags to sell or he would take them to the rag yard to raise money which he would then spend on Woodbine cigarettes.

Rationing continued and many foods were in short supply. The coasts were finally opened and people began to flock to the seaside. Mum and Dad were finding it difficult to make the money go round, but somehow they managed to take my brother Norman and me to a Butlins holiday camp. I cannot remember where it was but I think it may have been in Clacton. The holiday camps had started in the 1930s but closed during the war so they were still very much in their infancy and quite primitive. The chalets were similar to garden sheds and only contained beds crammed inside. The toilets and wash basins were in a nearby building. Brother Kenneth and the new baby, David, did not come with us; they stayed with Aunty Ann. This was the only holiday we ever had and Norman and I really enjoyed it. I had a couple of new dresses and a pair of sandals and Norman had new short trousers and a shirt. Norman and I were thrilled when we saw the sea for the first time – the vastness of all that water almost took our breath away. We played 'dare' with the playful waves that somersaulted and then receded, sucking at our toes as they sank into the sand. Dad sat in a deckchair and put a knot in each corner of his handkerchief and put it on his head. Mum lay on a towel and enjoyed the sunshine whilst Norman and I took our red metal buckets and wooden-handled spades and dug a big hole. We then made a sand-castle, putting the shells we had collected around the top and finishing it off with a moat we filled with water. Norman and I played for hours and made the biggest sandcastle ever and we were even more pleased when we won the sandcastle-making competition. We watched the swimming and knobbly knee contests and played rounders. We also enjoyed the food, apart from the curly white tripe when it was on the menu. I can remember feeling sick when I saw people eating this horrid stuff and Dad said it was a sheep's stomach and this made me feel even sicker than I already did.

When we returned home the reality soon hit Mum and Dad that there was not enough money to go around. Mum went to jumble sales or to the Portobello Road. The Portobello Road was at that time mainly made up of second-hand stalls. People spent time sorting through the old clothes that cost a few pennies and Mum rummaged around to try to find anything suitable for us children, but the clothes and shoes were always too big or too small. Mum cut our hair herself, putting a basin on our heads and cutting around it. One time she cut straight into my earlobe and it bled so much that even after it healed I was left with a scar.

One day, after the school summer break, I was late for school and hurried into the cloakroom. No one was in there and I put my hand into someone else's coat pocket and found a threepenny bit. I took it and hid it in my shoe until it was time to go home. The teacher asked the class if anyone had found it and I kept quiet. The girl who lost it was quite upset and I felt really sorry I had taken it, but was too afraid by now to admit what I had done. After school ended for the day I went to the newsagent's and sweet shop, I could not buy the sweets that were in the large jars as a ration book was needed for them so I bought myself a frozen Tizer-flavoured ice cube that I could suck until the flavour had gone or it had melted. You couldn't buy ice lollies in those days. Anyway, I felt disgusted with myself – this was stealing and I knew it was wrong to do this and I could not bring myself to lick the ice. I threw it into the curb side and trampled on it until there was nothing left. I spent weeks worrying as I thought the police were going to come and take me away for stealing the money.

Christmas came and went unnoticed. The winter months were harsh. I wore flimsy clothes and brown shoes with holes in the bottom that I stuffed with cardboard. The soles were hanging off like a crocodile's mouth, so I put elastic bands around to hold them together. I knew Mum could not afford to buy me or my brother new shoes. I also suffered with terrible cold infections and Mum gave me a square of rag to take to school to use as a hankie. When the rag was soaking wet from my runny nose I put it on the radiator. I expect I did a good job of spreading the germs around the classroom.

The rows between my father and grandmother were worse than ever and my mother was taking the brunt. Mum was too tired and weary to stand up for herself and Aunty Ann, who lived in Holland Park and had two sons named Rodney and Clifford, was just as bad; she seemed to add fuel to the fire by taking my mother's side against my father. Ann never confronted him but would tell Mum what she should do and say. Ann did not get on with her mother either so she also rowed with her. Mum was at her wit's end as she was pregnant again and did not know what to do for the best. There was always so much shouting and swearing going on I would go out of the house or hide just in case I got a whack around the head from Dad for being in the way.

The neighbours were also giving our family aggravation as Uncle George was getting worse and would stand in the street shouting and swearing at people as they walked by. The children in the street would tease him, which made him shout and wave his arms about even more. The kids had given him the name 'Dog End Dick', as he picked up dog ends and then smoked what was left of them or put the stubs in his pocket to undo and roll up later in his fag papers. The neighbours would call the police quite often from the red telephone box down our road, either because of George or because of the endless rows going on and noise. When the police had been and gone my grandmother would then give the man next door, Mr Shepherd, an ear bashing for calling the police. Mr Shepherd's wife was like a scared little rabbit and she would try to coax her husband indoors when they were nose to nose in verbal combat. Mr and Mrs Shepherd were the parents of one boy, John, and three girls, Sylvia, Pauline and Brenda. Mr Shepherd told his girls to stay away from all of us, including me, but seeing as we all walked to the same school this was a bit difficult, so we would meet up down the road when we were out of sight of their mum and dad.

One day when I was still only six years old, everyone was out apart from Uncle Billy, who was ten years older than me; Nan and George were also out so I went to play upstairs with my small black metal toy pram and ragdoll. I had found sixpence downstairs in the hallway and hidden it in the pram; I planned to buy an ounce of lemonade powder or sherbet from the corner shop later. It was nothing unusual to be left alone or for me to go out of the house alone. I had been to the park a few times with the girls next door. Sometimes we would pass men sitting on park benches and, supposedly oblivious to us girls, they would have their 'thingy' on show. We did not think anything of this: we were too young to know that it was wrong of them to do this, so we would just

19

titter and walk on. Anyway, on this particular day Billy found the sixpence in my pram.

'What is this doing in here?' he demanded, holding the sixpence between his fingers 'Where did you get it?'

I was too afraid to answer.

'I asked where you got this sixpence from. Answer me... or are you deaf?' he said, grabbing me by the shoulder.

His nose was almost touching mine. His face was twisted with anger. I had never seen him like this before and I said nothing as I was frozen with fear.

He twisted my arm up my back and marched me into the room which had a sink, gas stove and untidy metal bunk beds. He pulled down the blackout curtain and threw me onto the bottom bunk. I felt the rough blanket on my face and his weight on my chest. I tried to struggle free but it was useless – I could hardly breathe, I felt I was suffocating. Afterwards, when he had finished, he told me to get dressed and make myself look decent.

He put the blackout curtain back up and turned to me and said pleasantly, 'Rosie, I have decided I'm not going to tell your mum that you are a thief or she will call the police and you will be taken away and locked up for a very long time. So don't you worry – you can keep the sixpence and we will not mention anything to anyone about anything. Is that agreed?'

I nodded.

'I said, do we agree?' he pointed his finger at me as I cowered on the bed. 'You will not say a word to anyone, not ever. Now you promise me and I will promise you. I will not tell anyone you are a thief. Answer me, yes or no!'

'Yes,' I whispered.

Later that day when Mum came home I tried to say something to her but she brushed me aside.

'What is it, Rosie, what do you want now?' she said impatiently as she cradled Kenny who was crying very loudly.

I handed her the sixpence. 'I found this on the floor.'

'Oh thank you. I must have dropped it out of my purse earlier.' She placed Kenny onto the settee and put the six-pence into her pocket. She then hurriedly went towards the scullery. 'Keep an eye on Kenny for me as I have a lot to do, so don't bother me for now, there's a good girl'

Billy came down later just to make sure I hadn't said any-thing. When Mum was out of sight he put his finger to his lips. 'Shush. Keep your mouth shut and not a word to anyone or else you know what will happen – you will be taken away!'

I stood frozen to the spot until he left the room.

Chapter 4

Grandmother, Nancy Bolch, whom I have referred to as Nan, must have previously lived in a large house as she and Pop had so many possessions and furniture crammed into the upstairs flat that you could not get from one side of the room to the other. When Mum and Dad were out, Nan persuaded Pop and George to help her to shift furniture and boxes out into the back garden. The garden was soon overflowing and the neighbours were very upset about the mountain accumulating and complained bitterly to my father, saying this could attract rats and if it was not cleared they were going to report us to the authorities. Dad was so angry he forbade Nan, George and Pop to come downstairs ever again. Mum agreed with this and threatened that if they came downstairs again they would get a bucket of water thrown over them. I would have a good ransack in the garden, as did the many insects that were crawling all over the papers and books. I even found an old wooden wind-up gramophone with a horn. I brought the gramophone indoors and hid it under my bed intending to play it later, when no one would be in. But the records were cylinders and they crumbled in my hands when I tried to play them.

One cold, bitter, winter's day I came home from school and found Pop sitting by the fire. My hands and feet were numb with the cold. 'You know you are not allowed down here Pop,' I said angrily, 'and I'm cold and you're taking up all the warmth from the fire with your head almost up the chimney.'

Pop began to cough. 'Go away, clear off and mind your own business.'

'If you don't move, I am going to throw a bucket of water over you, like Mum said she would do if you came down here again.'

'I told you to clear off,' he coughed. 'Go on, hop it and leave me alone.'

I went into the scullery and stood on a chair and half-filled a bucket with water. I then struggled into the sitting room and threw the cold water over Pop then dropped the bucket and ran. My mum caught hold of me along the passageway.

'What have you been up to, Rosie?' she said angrily as she heard Pop cursing as he followed after me dripping with water.

'She threw a bucket of water over me. That's what she did. Look at me – I am soaked.'

Mum held on to me. 'What did you do that for, you bad girl?' she shouted.

I started to cry. 'But that is what you said you would do if any of them from upstairs came down here and I was just doing what you said.'

'I only said that, but I wouldn't really do it, you stupid girl.'

'But I didn't know, did I?' I sobbed, but Mum would not listen. I had never seen her so angry. She wrapped a towel around Pop and, after drying him, sat him by the fire and then made him a cup of tea. I sat quietly crying in a corner. Pop was wheezing and coughing even more when the smoke from the fire blew back into the room as the chimney had never been swept, and when the front door opened, it acted like a wind tunnel.

One morning, a week later, I was just on my way out of the

door to go to school when Pop called down to me to come upstairs to see him. He was standing in the kitchen and trying to talk to me in between coughing bouts, but I could not understand what he was trying to say. I noticed he was blue around his mouth. Pop could not stop his coughing so he waved his hand for me to go. I wanted to say sorry for throwing water at him but could not find the words. He patted me on the head and gestured me again to go.

He died that day and my mother said later in anger that it was my fault; I had killed him by throwing the water over him, turning his bronchitis into pneumonia.

Pop had a pauper's funeral. We children were not allowed to attend.

At the age of nine years old I was not only wicked; I had now become a murderer.

Chapter 5

Uncle George was an average-built man of about five foot nine. He had a slim face, thin lips a straight nose and light-brown hair. He once had a career in journalism until he suffered a nervous breakdown caused by bomb shock at the beginning of the war.

Mum said a mirror had fallen from the wall and shattered, which sent George into a frenzy and he went to the police station and told them he had killed his schoolteacher. But as he had left school some time ago it was obvious to everyone that George had had a breakdown. Other than that, George was a very clever man; he was a genius at shorthand writing and mathematics. He spent hours sitting at the top of the stairs with his notebooks writing, drawing maps or writing music notes. He must have heard music in his head to be able to write like he did. Where Nan was concerned George acted like an obedient dog; he was at her beck and call. He would wait eagerly for her next command, even if it was to go on a mission to find a shop open on a Sunday (only newsagents' were allowed to open on a Sunday) or on a Thursday afternoon when they would be closed in our area. A short bus ride away the shops closed on a Wednesday afternoon and would be open on Thursdays, not that George ever went on the bus, as he would walk everywhere. He had a terrific memory and would be able to tell you all the street names for miles around. George wore two or three shirts at the same time and three pairs of trousers under a short jacket and his trousers were tied up with string. I asked him one day why did he wear all his clothes at once and he said because he did not want to lose them. Nan wrote lots of letters but she did not trust the local post box to be emptied on time so George would walk the two miles to the sorting office to post her letters. He seemed to enjoy being on a mission and doing whatever she wanted.

Nan would sometimes take me to the theatre with her, either in London or at Windsor. She would spend the early morning getting ready; she put on a little lipstick, pinched her cheeks, then put on her best clothes and hat. I looked forward to these trips to the theatre and my heart always jumped a beat when the orchestra was warming up in the pit. Nan also loved opera and French films. I found out later in life that she had had a French grandmother.

Grandmother Nancy's maiden name was Beales. She was born in Kensington, London. The Beales family originated in Kensal Town, which was, at one time, a village just outside London. Nancy's family were quite well off, possibly by inheriting money from her grandparents, Samuel and his wife, Amelia. Her father, Arthur, was a self-educated man and dedicated to reading philosophy and English classics. He married twice. The second wife was a girl from a gypsy family – this was Nancy's mother – and they had eight children. Nancy had a good upbringing and a very good education but she threw it all away when she married someone considered by her family to be an uneducated, poor man – my grandfather Augustus Bolch. My grandmother lived to regret this marriage, as being poor in those days was very serious. Nancy was a free-spirited person, a trait possibly inherited from her mother. Despite their poverty, they had four children, my mother being the eldest. Nancy had no idea how to do domestic chores or look after her children and would quite often leave them and move somewhere else still owing the rent money. Her husband and the children walked the streets sometimes to try to find her. Aunty Ann never forgave her mother for not caring enough and she never had a good word to say about her.

Despite the strange ways Nan had, I was fascinated by her; she seemed to live in her own little cocoon. She was quite happy in her world and would hum and sing as if she did not have a care in the world. She did not take any notice about what people might say about her and she could hold her own in any argument if anyone was brave enough to challenge her. Nan may have come from a good family background but she could certainly 'eff and blind' and tell people 'to get out of the bleeding way' or to 'bugger off'. Every day she would give George a bag of crumbs to throw out for the birds, but he was told to throw it into the road outside the house next door as she did not want the birds messing outside our house. This would really annoy the neighbours in the house on the other side from the Shepherds. Two sisters lived there and Nan referred to them as 'Armhole', as the poor woman could not lift her arm, and 'Eagle Beak', as Nan considered her to be nosey and always looking out from her window. Nan said it was like 'cannons to the left of her and cannons to the right', living in the middle of these people.

Although Nan was offhand to everybody, she was always kind to me and would say I was beautiful. She liked cooking for herself and when she went out she always had a tuck bag. If she boiled eggs, she only ate the yolk and George would have the rest; if she cooked rhubarb, then she would pour the juice into a cup and give it to me saying it was ruby wine. Although Nan never spoke about her family, she did once take me to meet her sister 'Ciss' at Kensal Rise, or we would visit her brother-in-law who lived near the Portobello Road. I think his name was Albert. He had one leg shorter than the other and wore a black built-up shoe. We would arrive just as they would be serving afternoon tea so we would be able to have a sandwich and piece of cake if we were lucky, but I had the feeling that she was not really welcomed by them.

Although I was quite content to be with Nan and looked forward to seeing her, I was otherwise very unhappy and felt isolated as Dad was not around much (and when he was I tried to stay out of the way) and Mum was always busy with the children. In bed at night I had a dream that would come back to me again and again. I would be in a train going across an iron bridge, which I presumed was the Tyne Bridge, and the train left the track and plunged into the river with the deafening sound of screeching as iron scraped upon iron. Then I was in the freezing water being washed downstream. It was very dark and I could hardly catch my breath as I was bobbing up and down and pushing bodies out of my way as they tried to cling to me. I saw the outline of the carriages sinking, then I went under the black water. I would wake up crying, shaking and trembling.

Chapter 6

Times may have been tough in post-war Britain for our family, but it was just the way things were then. My mother Helen was a very well-read, intelligent woman who by circumstance did not reach her potential. Mum always did the best she could for us all but her growing family and the lack of money stretched her to the limit. When she did have some spare money she would give us a treat by taking us to the cinema, which she really enjoyed. We queued for sometimes up to an hour to get in and we would often miss the beginning of the B film and other times we were split up into different seats. The A film always followed the interval and the Pathé News.

The only way I can describe my mother is that she was round; she had a round face, round body, and often a round belly from pregnancy. Her eyes were dark and active and she did not miss much of what was going on around her. Her short, dark-brown hair was held back with a hair clip. When indoors Mum wore a flowery, full-length wraparound apron. Monday was washday, and woe betide any housewife if they were to put washing out on a Sunday as this was considered to be a sin. On Fridays Mum would clean and whiten the doorstep, with what looked like a white stone brick dipped in water.

When Aunty Ann visited us Mum and her would talk about

worldly subjects and give opinions on anything from politics to everyday humdrum things like the price of bread or milk. Mum did not smoke but many people around her did, including Aunty Ann and Dad. What with their smoking, the London smog and the smoke billowing down the chimney, it was no wonder that Mum had a terrible cough; sometimes she would cough that much she was sick. This cough would last right through winter and into late spring.

Saturday was always a busy shopping day as the shops did not open on Sundays. Mum spent the whole of Saturday afternoons going from one shop to another looking for bargains with what little money she had. She stopped to chat to some of the neighbours but was always guarded in what she said, and we were told not to tell people our business should they ask us any questions. On Mum's Saturday shopping trips she always ended up at the butcher's, asking him for cheap leftover meat, the bakery for stale cakes and bread, and the greengrocers for over-ripe fruit and vegetables, what Mum would call 'specs'. She piled all the rotten, green, furry oranges and brown, bad apples, speckled greens, mud-covered potatoes and a sad-looking cauliflower, and any other so-called bargains onto the pushchair. One shopkeeper, if Mum was lucky, would save her some cracked eggs. My brothers and I looked forward to her coming home on Saturday evenings as we would sort out the best of the fruit, cut off the brown halves of the apples and the furry, green sides of the oranges and stuff our faces with the fruit, followed by the stale cake and bread. We feasted like royalty. Sometimes Mum would make a spotted dick with flour, suet and currants, all mixed together in a basin, then tie it up in a dishcloth and boil it in water for about an hour. This pudding was delicious and filled us up.

Money, or the lack of it, had become a big problem, so I no longer had my dinner at school. Instead, I walked home at lunchtime and had a slice of bread and jam before going back in the afternoon, often arriving late, and after being told off had to stay in an extra half-hour after school as detention.

I often played on my own, sliding down the banister and ending up with a bump against the round wooden ball at the bottom, then I'd run up the stairs and slide down again. Uncle George would sit there taking no notice of me; he would carry on doing his writing or smoking a fag and flicking the ash off whilst deep in thought. One day he had been told by Nan to sit at the bottom of the stairs and not to annoy her whilst she was busy. I was engaged in this actively of sliding down the banisters when I heard Nan singing and I went to have a peep over the top of the stairs. Nan was standing in the nude, at a table that was covered with a blanket, doing her ironing; I sat very quietly on the top stair to watch her. Now and again she spat on the black flat iron that she was heating on the gas stove – if it sizzled it was hot enough to carry on. Then she turned her garment over and ironed the other side. After she had inspected the dress she was working on she hung it over a chair, filled a bowl with water and washed herself all over with a flannel and soap, and then she put her best clothes on. Nan looked very pleased with herself because it was Thursday and she would be going to the Royal Windsor Theatre, as she did regularly. Nan did not notice me watching as her deft fingers worked on her hair, pinning it into a bun at the back of her neck. She worked in the odd stray strands, then she put on her coat and fox-fur wrap, her best hat and shoes and checked her lipstick and pinched her cheeks to give then a pink glow. She looked amazing, just like a well-to-do lady; no one would ever guess, on this one day of the week, where she was coming from. When Nan was ready to leave she picked up her handbag and a carrier bag that she had filled with 'tuck', the food she would take with her to eat later.

She saw me studying her. 'Hello, Rosie, what are you doing up here? I hope you haven't come up here to ransack.' She shooed me down the stairs before she hurried out of the front door.

George was then off duty and he had a little peace to be able to do his writing. Later I heard him go out of the house on his regular mission to find dog ends. No one was in the house so, out of curiosity, I decided I would go to have a look around upstairs. I crept up, turned right, up the few more stairs on the landing and tiptoed along to the room at the front of the house. I peeped around the door, then ventured inside and quietly shut the door behind me. The room was stacked with furniture and cardboard boxes and wooden tea chests, containing all sorts of things. A piano was covered with a sheet and with lots of books and papers piled high on the top. I lifted the lid and pressed one note and slammed it shut again. There was hardly space to move around in this room. After I had rummaged around and nosed in the boxes to see what was of interest, my attention took me over to the fireplace and the glass-domed clock with gold figurines holding a chime. I was fascinated, too, by the brass gas lights that were on either side of the mantelpiece; I knew Nan still used these as she sent George to the corner shop every now and again to buy new filaments. I suddenly heard a noise and ducked down behind a box. Someone entered the room so I tried to creep on my knees along the floor hoping I could get to the door unseen. I knocked something over so I stood up and tried to run to the doorway, but Billy barred my way. I felt a shiver down my spine.

'What are you doing up here?'

I tried to run past him but he grabbed hold of me. 'What's your hurry?'

I kicked out at his leg. Billy laughed and held me tight as I struggled and kicked. He tickled me under the arms trying to make me laugh, whilst still holding me tight.

'I said, what's your hurry and what are you doing up here?'

I fell onto the floor, still kicking out at him. Billy knelt down and roughly took my shoes off and tickled my feet 'Proper little spitfire, aren't you? What do we do with naughty girls, eh?' I felt could take no more of this. I found nothing to laugh about.

'Stop it!' I screamed, kicking and struggling, as his fingers dug painfully into my ankles. 'Get off of me! Leave me alone!' I cried, growing weaker and breathless.

'What will you do if I stop?' he asked, laughing. 'Go on, tell me. What will you do if I stop?' I could hardly catch my breath. 'Go on, tell me,' he repeated.

'Stop it, stop, Billy; I've had enough.' He stopped tickling and was on top of me in a flash, rummaging at the same time with his flies. I could do no more, I was too exhausted. I had no option but to let him do as he wished.

Afterwards he put a sixpence in my hand and told me to get up and tidy myself and to go downstairs before anyone came home.

'Don't forget what I told you. Not a word to anyone as you know what will happen to you if you do.'

I felt ashamed and dirty and realized there was nothing I could do but to keep quiet.

Chapter 7

Even though the war had been over for a few years, little had changed – rationing was still in place and there was still a shortage of most everyday needs. Owing to the shortage of food, allotments had become very popular. People grew their vegetables and fruit on the allotments and then would exchange their excess produce with each other, but Mum and Dad did not have the means or time to run an allotment so we had to make do with the leftover fruit from the greengrocer's on a Saturday evening, just before closing time. Clothing was also in short supply and women had to make do and mend. The evenings were spent listening to the wireless whilst the housewives did sewing and knitting. Mum enjoyed listening to *Dick Barton – Special Agent* and Dad to the news and sports results.

Mum had hardly any money and I had no shoes to wear so she kept me away from school for a few days, but then she became worried when the School Board man came to the house to ask why I was not at school. Mum told him I had been unwell but I would be back at school the following day. Mum found an old pair of black Wellington boots that were a few sizes too big for me and she said they would do for now.

'No one will notice you don't have any socks on,' she reasoned. 'And it will be only for a few days until I get some money from your father.'

I went back to school and was caught talking in class to another girl. The teacher walked very slowly up to my desk.

'And what is more important, Rose Handleigh, than what I have to say?' she said in an even tone. A wave of fear enveloped me when she screamed, 'Get to my desk right now.'

The class was in total silence and all eyes followed me as I made my way to the front of the class. The teacher grabbed me by the shoulders and shook me until I thought my brains and teeth would fall out.

'I will teach you a lesson to listen to me when I am talking,' she breathlessly ranted. 'You are going to grow up knowing nothing and will amount to nothing either.' That hollow-cheeked, black-eyed, tweedy woman then ordered me to kneel on the floor facing her. All the morning I knelt uncomfortably on the hard, wooden flooring. My head was throbbing and my nose running as I quietly whimpered. When I was eventually told to stand up my legs almost buckled under me with pain. At the backs of my thighs the Wellington boots had dug into me, leaving my legs red and sore. The teacher noticed my painful legs and gave a self-satisfied smirk. I hated the teachers and the way they got away with so much cruelty to us children. We never told our parents what the teachers did to us. If we had done so, our parents would have taken no notice as it was considered to be none of their business what went on during school time. So the teachers had a free rein to inflict their evil punishments upon us.

There was much excitement one afternoon in the school. Apparently the Americans had heard that the British people were starving and suffering with hunger, so they had sent food parcels to give to the children in the schools. The children were told to all wait outside the classroom and to come in one at a time with our eyes closed. It was ages until it was my turn to enter the classroom, I made my way to the desk with my eyes shut tight and was instructed to point my finger downwards. I did so and my finger came to rest on a packet of custard powder. I was disappointed as the other children from my class had picked out tins of Spam, corned beef and large packets of biscuits. Nevertheless I thought my mum would be pleased. I rushed into the house and proudly gave the packet of custard powder to her.

'Custard powder!' she bellowed. 'What the bloody hell do I want with a packet of custard? It means I will have to buy extra milk and use up my rations for the sugar. Bloody custard powder, I ask you! What a bleeding stupid thing to bring home.'

I felt so ashamed that I was not able to give her something more exciting and thought that this was my punishment for being a bad person.

As well as a shortage of food and clothing, there was also a shortage of coal. One freezing-cold day Norman and I trailed behind Mum, struggling to help push the empty pram across the fallen snow that had now turned to ice under our feet, as we walked the two or three miles to the coal depot. When we arrived we joined the long line of people to await our turn to be served, which turned out to be over an hour later. I was wearing sandals and a thin jacket over a cotton dress and Norman was in his short trousers and grey jacket. We were stamping our feet and shaking our hands to try to get warm. Our breath hung in the air like a swirl from a cigarette. When it was our turn, Mum was a few pennies short and her eyes filled with tears. The coalman, with a hessian sack cut up one seam covering his head to keep the coal dust from his hair, took pity and told Mum that it was all right, she could owe it to him. He then helped to put a sack of coal into the pram. He turned his blackened face to Norman and me, so that we could see the whites of his eyes and his teeth, and then he smiled.

'You take good care of your mum, kids, and be good to her.'

Mum thanked him. The walk home was almost impossible. Mum, Norman and I pushed the pram as best we could. It was now twice as heavy with the sack of coal in it, and the snow was now coming down so heavy we could hardly see what was in front of us. We were so relieved when we finally arrived home. That evening Dad rolled newspaper into balls and put sticks of wood on the top. When it was burning nicely he put the wet coal on, which quickly put the fire out. After a few more attempts the fire was burning well again. When anyone came in the front door, the smoke billowed back into the room and Dad shouted along the hallway: 'Hurry up and shut that bloody door, will you?' The coal did not last for long but it warmed up this one room nicely. The rest of the house remained icy cold.

One day Nan had another big row with Dad. I don't even know what it was about or how it started but she accused Dad of starving us children whilst he went to the club buying booze for himself and his cronies and then pissed the money against the wall. There may have been some truth in this accusation as Mum scrimped and scraped to get by, but Dad assured Mum that as a working man he deserved to go for a pint at the end of the week. It was not long after this that Mum and Dad received a summons to attend the court to answer a charge of child neglect. Nan had instigated this; she had gone to the courts to report them for not feeding and caring for us. There was an almighty row between Nan and Dad and poor Mum could not stop weeping. George sat as usual on the top of the stairs, looking on with a stupid grin on his face; Billy was leaning over the top banister to watch the action. Insults and swearing were exchanged for about ten minutes, Dad at the bottom of the stairs and Nan at the top. Nan retreated into her room with a loud bang of her door behind her. Dad shouted for all to hear, 'I'll swing for her' (meaning he would kill her and hang for her), and then he marched back to the sitting room, slamming the door with an almighty force. On the day we attended court Mum dressed me in nice new, turn-down, short socks with a pink border around the top and a skirt and blouse. She had washed and then combed the tangles out of our hair and made us all look clean and presentable. Mum wore her best blue floral dress and navy hat and she told us children that when someone asked if we were well fed we were to say 'yes', otherwise we would end up in a children's home. Dad looked smart in his navy-blue suit and trilby hat. The magistrate's court was only a few streets away from our road and Mum was thankful it was sunny and not raining as we did not have coats to wear. My parents went into the court first and stood side by side facing the judge. Nan went into the witness box and told the court that we children were not cared for properly and we were not fed either, as her son-in-law, Norman Handleigh, spent all the money in the pub. Norman, Kenneth, me and a policewoman holding David's hand were asked to come in. People in the courtroom were looking at us as if we were freaks and I felt a wave of terror spread through me. I did not want to leave my mum and dad and live in the children's home. My brothers stood like little tin soldiers with their arms held stiffly by their sides, David looked as if he wanted to cry when he saw Mum, but he just sniffed back his runny nose. The potatoes and bread had filled me out so I did not look as if I was starving but my brothers looked very thin, pale and run down. The judge kindly said 'Hello' to us and beckoned us with his fat fingers to come forward. I thought the well-dressed suited man must have been like a king, as he was sitting on what I believed to be a wooden throne. He put down his fountain pen, adjusted the large round dark glasses on his hooked nose, studied the papers on his desk for a few moments, then slowly studied us one at a time. We were shaking and I heard Norman's teeth chattering.

'Don't be frightened. No one is going to hurt you; I just want to ask you a few questions.' We did not respond. He continued 'Firstly, do you believe in God?' We nodded. 'Do you know what telling the truth means?' We nodded again. 'Can you remember what you had for dinner yesterday?' We did not answer. 'Well, can you tell me what you had for breakfast this morning?' Again we did not answer. The judge could see he was not getting anywhere with us so we were asked to go and sit down on the wooden bench at the side of the courtroom.

The judge then listened to Dad explaining that his mother-in-law, Nancy Bolch, and he, had a running disagreement and that she was always poking her nose into their family life and would not let them live in peace. After some deliberation the judge ordered that we were to be given malt and orange juice. Someone in the courtroom gave Mum four tins of the malt and some tokens for the national health orange juice. We children did not mind this at all as we liked the orange juice and the malt was runny, like toffee, and tasted sweet.

One day, almost a year later, I came home from school and rushed into the toilet next to the scullery. George was in there doing a wee. I must have startled him as he turned in mid-stream and said, 'Get the fuck out or I'll piss all over you.' With that he did piss all over my dress. I was so shocked that before I could say anything George turned and ran out. I cried out after him 'You dirty bleeder. What did you do that for? You have no right to be downstairs in our toilet.' I was crying and felt humiliated. I held up the hem of my sopping wet, smelly dress. Mum came rushing along the passage towards the scullery. George pushed pass her and ran up the stairs with my mother swearing and shouting at him. Nan was not at home when all this happened. When Dad came home, Mum was still very angry and told him what George had done. With that my dad did no more – he went straight to the police station to report George for assault.

Chapter 8

Nan did not have a clue about what had happened until she read the summons that George had received for him to attend court to answer to an allegation of assault against me. Nan tried to find out what it was all about by asking Mum but she would not tell her.

A few days before the court case Nan asked my mother if she could take me to see a musical. Foolishly, my mother agreed on the condition that she did not pump me for information about the court case and she was not to ask me any questions at all.

Nan took me to Piccadilly Circus. There seemed to be hundreds of people there. Some were sitting on the steps below the statue of Eros just talking and taking in the sights. Taxis clogged the roads and double-decker buses rolled along every few minutes. I was mesmerized and excited by all the sights and sounds. I had never seen so many coloured flashing lights on the buildings advertising various products, Wrigley chewing gum and Coca-Cola bottles that seemed to move from side to side. There was flickering lights of a pelican balancing a pint glass of Guinness on his beak, then the lights faded before other lights showed the slogan 'My goodness my Guinness'. There was so much hustle and bustle of people hurrying by – the buses, the cars, the tourists, the atmosphere – everything was very exciting to me and I enjoyed every minute.

Nan was walking beside me when she suddenly stopped and turned towards me and said, 'Tell me what Georgie has done to you.'

'No I can't,' I replied. 'Mum and Dad said I am not to tell you anything.'

'Then in that case I am going to leave you here to find your own way back home.'

'But I haven't got any money for the bus fare home,' I wailed.

'Then in that case tell me what he has done.'

'No!' I said defiantly.

She started to walk away from me. People were hurrying pass and she would soon be lost in the crowd. I was so afraid of being left there in the middle of London with no way to get home. I began to panic.

'He hit me!' I shouted.

She came back. 'Now that was not hard to tell me, was it?'

Nan did not say any more about it and we did go to see a musical. I think Nan was hoping by the time I got home I would have forgotten about her asking me questions. I did not tell Mum that Nan had asked me to tell her about what George had done or that she had said she would leave me in the centre of London if I didn't tell her. There would have been another big row and I would be the reason why, so it was better for me to keep quiet.

On the day of the court case I had to stand once again near the bench to tell the judge what had happened.

'Did he say anything when he wet your dress?' he asked.

'Yes,' I replied softly.

'And what was it? What did he say to you?'

'I can't tell you; it's rude.'

'Come and whisper in my ear what he said and no one else will hear what you have to say.'

There were a lot of official-looking people straining their

ears to try to hear what I would have to say. I stood on tiptoe and whispered in the judge's ear: 'He said he would fucking piss all over me if I did not get out.'

Poor George had been told what to say by Nan and so he rambled on about it was not him that had hit me; it was the boy that lived next door. When the judge heard what George was saying and it did not make sense or relate to what he was being accused of, he ordered that George be sent for psychiatric assessment in a mental institution. I felt awful about this and thought he did not deserve this to happen to him. It was only a pee and he had not hurt me not like his brother Billy had. I hated myself for helping to put George away. George was locked up for months and then he was put on probation.

A few days after the court case, Nan was waiting for me to come in the front door. She stood at the bottom of the stairs. I felt nervous as to what she would say or do to me.

'Come here, Rosie,' she said in an over-friendly voice. She had a small cardboard box in her hand. She held it tight at both ends. 'Come here and look at this.' She beckoned me to come nearer. I edged nearer to see what she had. It was a box of marshmallows, still wrapped in Cellophane, and there was a shiny picture of the marshmallows on the front.

'Come,' she said, 'take one of the marshmallows.' She held on tightly to the box with both hands as she offered it to me. 'Go on, take one.'

I pretended to take one from the picture. 'Go on put it in your mouth.' I went along with this and pretended to put the sweet into my mouth.

'Can you taste how good it is? Can you taste how soft and sweet it is?'

'No I can't,' I replied, puzzled.

'No and you are not going to either. You bad, naughty girl!' With that she turned and hurried up the stairs. She never mentioned anything to do with the court case again and it was a long time before she even spoke to me again.

The probation officer came one day to see my grandmother to talk about George before he was due to be released. Nan gave him such a hard-luck story about how she couldn't do anything as she was too ill with worry; she couldn't even clean the windows or do the shopping and no one would lift a finger to help her. The probation officer felt so sorry that he filled a bucket with water and rolled up his sleeves and washed the windows inside and out. I don't think they had ever been washed before.

In the meantime Billy had got away with a lot worse but I was too ashamed and afraid to tell anyone about this secret. I was convinced more than ever that I was a bad person as it was my fault entirely for letting Billy do what he did to me, and it was my fault for stealing and my fault that Pop had died.

I was so miserable and unhappy I started to take my anger out on my brothers by hitting them until they cried. Poor Mum did not know what to do about me when I was bullying them so much.

It was a few months after George came home that the strain of all that had happened and the continuing rows finally made Dad decide he had had enough and he left to live with his friend from the Working Men's Club. A few days later I came straight home from school instead of lingering like I normally did. George let me in. I went along the passageway towards the back of the house and noticed the scullery door was closed – it was never closed and I could smell something strange. I opened the door. The room was filled with gas. I rushed in and quickly opened the door leading to the side alleyway. Mum was on the floor with her head in the gas oven. I turned the gas off and pulled Mum out; she was barely conscious and in my haste to pull her out from the oven she fell sideways, knocking over a bowl of water that had been on a stool, all over her and the floor. I grabbed a tea towel and waved it around to try to clear the gas out. Mum sat up coughing and choking.

I fell to the floor beside her and started to cry. 'What have you done, Mum? Why have you done this? Do you want to leave us?' I sobbed even more and my eyes and head felt heavy.

'Don't cry,' she said, putting her arm around me and laughing and crying at the same time. 'Mummy is only playing. Don't be silly – I'm not going to leave you.'

Later, when my brothers came home, Mum took us all to the house where Dad was staying. He looked shocked to see us all standing there on the doorstep. He invited us in as if we were strangers. We children went into a different room whilst they chatted. I don't know what was said but Dad came home with us. He never found out what Mum had tried to do in the scullery and I never breathed a word to anyone either.

Billy, in the meantime, was forever on the prowl looking for me when no one was around. He seemed to pop up from nowhere when I thought he was out of the house. He would then either twist my arm up my back or pin me down with his knees on my shoulders and dig his fingers into my ribcage until I submitted. In the end I found it was far easier to give in to him than to be treated to this torture. I was convinced it was too late to tell anyone and, as I had not put up any resistance, I was as much to blame as Billy. I thought if my dad was to find out about Billy there would be so much trouble and Dad would whack me and put me in a children's home. I was feeling more and more alone and weighed down with the heavy burden of secrets and guilt.

Chapter 9

Our mother went in and out of hospital many times with miscarriages; she also had two or three stillborn babies and another boy, Robert, who lived for just a few days. Sometimes, when Mum was in hospital, I would stay in North Finchley with my Great-Aunty Ethel and Uncle Ted, a warm, loving couple who always made us feel welcome. Great-Aunt Ethel was my dad's aunty; she reminded me a great deal of my grandmother Rose; her accent was still strong Geordie and she chuckled and laughed, just like my grandmother did. Uncle Ted, who was a slim, balding, bespectacled man who sucked and puffed on his pipe in between telling me stories about the Handleigh family members. He took great pride in his knowledge of the Handleigh family and could name every Handleigh in Britain. He explained to me my great, great-grandfather Edward had changed his name from Handley to Handleigh for some unknown reason and all the people with this spelling of Handleigh were related. Aunt Ethel and Uncle Ted lived in a three-storey apartment above a bank in the High Street. To get to the flat we had to go around to an alleyway at the back of the High Street and up some iron steps leading from the garden that was overflowing with mint growing wild. Aunt Ethel always prepared a lovely tea of fish-paste sandwiches, lettuce, celery, spring onions and apple pie with evaporated milk and also Victoria sponge cake filled with butter icing and jam, all served on pretty patterned china on a lovely damask tablecloth. I stayed with them without my brothers, as it would have been too much for them to look after us all. I enjoyed being spoilt by them. Aunt Ethel insisted I had a bath every evening before bedtime, which was unheard of at home as we only had wash-downs from a bowl of water or a dip now and again in a tin bath. One day Aunt Ethel showed me a newspaper cutting from the 1930s showing a picture of an alderman in his chain of office, sitting next to King George V and Queen Mary in an open coach with horses waving to the crowd on a visit to Newcastle. I think Aunt Ethel said it was her father but I could not find out any more about this from my father. When it was time for me to leave, my dad would come to collect me and Aunty and Uncle would always give me a shilling.

When I was unable to go to my aunt and uncle in Finchley, I joined my brothers and we stayed with Aunty Ann, who was a different sort of person altogether. Ann lived in Holland Park with her husband, Len, their two sons, Rodney and Clifford, and a younger daughter named Marion. Aunty Ann, unlike my mother, was slim and stylish. Her dark hair was sometimes worn in a turban to cover her curlers which she took out in the evening before Len came home from work; she also had grey-green eyes just like her mother and she had a severe hard-looking face that matched her despotic personality. Ann smoked a lot, especially when drinking her numerous cups of tea made with sterilized milk. When she was thinking she grimaced or would purse her lips in an unsmiling smile. Aunty Ann, like her mother, was someone you did not mess with; she had such a sharp tongue we would be careful not to upset her and we all walked on eggshells when she was around.

In the mornings Aunty Ann would give my brothers and me a sandwich of bread and jam wrapped up in newspaper, a threepenny bit (or, if we were lucky, a sixpence), then she'd chuck us out of the front door telling us we were not to come back for the rest of the day. If we did come back too early, she refused to let us in the house. We would have to sit on the doorstep, raining or not, until she decided we could come in.

My brothers and I walked to the large pond in Kensington Gardens with fishing nets we had made with bamboo sticks, wire and rag or net from old curtains. Empty jam jars, with handles made with string, would carry the stickleback fish we caught. We took extra jars so we could sell the fish for threepence to the posh kids. We then played on the swings and roundabouts and then we would raid the litter bins for empty lemonade or Tizer bottles that we could take to the grocery shop to exchange for a few pence each.

In the evening Aunty Ann gave us mash potatoes and gravy. We were made to lick the plate clean and then she would put stewed apple onto the same plate. If the plate was not licked clean then the stewed apple would mingle with the gravy and we were still told to lick the plate clean. This, Aunty Ann said, was to save on the washing up. Aunty Ann never said a kind word to me and I think she was pleased when we all went home after she had done her sisterly duty by looking after us.

Sometimes Mum came with us to Kensington Gardens or to Regent's Park, where we would be treated to a half-hour on a rowing boat on the Serpentine and an ice-lolly. Then Mum played ball with us, in amongst the lovely big old trees. We then fell breathless onto the grass and Mum gave us sandwiches and homemade lemonade.

Chapter 10

Back at St John's Avenue my brothers and I had made friends with some of the other children who lived in the road, all except the three boys from the Cobb family, who lived opposite us and who were forever tormenting George and calling us names and telling the other children not to play with us as we had fleas. They changed our surname, Handleigh, to Hanpots, as they said we were all potty. Well, I don't know about being potty, but it was certainly true about the fleas; I was an expert at picking them off of my legs and squashing them between my thumbnails. The Cobbs had a horrible sandy-coloured dog named Rover that would either bite you or hump your legs. Dogs were not restricted to only being out with their owners and many people would let the dogs out in the morning and they would meet up with other dogs and roam the streets in packs and mess on the pavements. Rover was no exception. Some days he would lay in wait behind the hedge for a car to pass by and jump out and run and bark behind it or he would do the same to anyone riding their bike on their way to work. Many cyclists were startled by Rover barking and biting at the wheels and they would try to kick him away only to come tumbling off into the road. Next door but one to the Cobbs lived their cousins, the Canty family. They seemed to keep themselves to themselves and old Mrs Canty, the grandmother, lived upstairs and would always refer to me as 'Rose-a-day'. Sometimes when we children were bored on a rainy or cold dark evening, Mum would give me some pennies and ask me to go and see if the Canty boy would sell me some old comics, like the *Beano* and *Dandy*. The boy let me buy them at two for a penny. I'm sure the comics helped me to learn to read well. I desperately wanted to know what the characters were saying in the balloon boxes above their heads and pestered Mum to teach me to read what they said. Mum also told us fairy stories and made up some of her own about princes and princesses who lived in lovely palaces.

Other children, all except the Shepherds and Cobbs, seemed to be quite all right about playing with us. We played with marbles on the drain-hole cover outside our house or played Tin Can Alley, where one child would throw an old can down the road and, whilst they went to retrieve it, we would all hide in front gardens behind the hedges and then the one who had the tin would have to find us before we could run out and kick the tin. Other times we had fun making go-karts out of orange boxes and old pram wheels and we would then race them down the road. We thought it was great fun to play Knock Down Ginger, where we would knock on people's front door and run away before they answered. My brothers and I often went fishing for stickle-backs in the Grand Canal. One day my brother Kenny fell in and I stood on the bank side screaming until a teenage boy heard my cries and jumped in and dragged Kenny out. This happened when Mum was in hospital; the boy who saved Ken took us home safely. Kenny was soaking wet and he was shivering. My dad rewarded the boy with two and sixpence. But he did not tell Mum what had happened as he did not want her to worry.

I made friends with a girl named Irene, who lived across the road with her mother and grandmother. I thought she was really pleasant, clever and talented. Irene wore pretty clothes and I envied her being able to attend dancing lessons. She had lovely black tap and pink ballet shoes. After her dance lessons in the church hall, Irene would show me what she had learnt, and then I would try to do the dances like she had shown me, including the Scottish jig over a white chalk cross we had drawn on the pavement. Irene even invited me to her birthday party once and we played Pass the Parcel, Postman's Knock and Musical Chairs.

Unfortunately I was becoming quite a bully to some of the children in our road. One girl, Deidre, who lived down the bottom of the road, was a really pleasant girl, yet I would shout and intimidate her, just because I could. I was spiteful to my brothers and gave them a good thumping sometimes. I also joined other children in brick and stone fights on the bomb sites, and it was a wonder we did not have a serious injury with all those missiles flying about.

A quiet family – mother, father and two teenage children – lived a few doors further down our road. They belonged to the Salvation Army and every Sunday morning, wearing their uniforms, would pass our house on their way to their meeting place. I marched behind them for fun reciting, 'Salvation Army all gone barmy. Excepting the leader and he's a bleeder.' They never said a word to me; they just marched on with their eyes focused steadily in front of them.

I was still friends with Sylvia Shepherd and one day we decided to explore to see where different roads led to. We were gone quite a long time, as we stopped at the black-smith's to see the cart horses being shoed before heading back, and as we walked up the road we could see Sylvia's mum and dad waiting on the doorstep. When we drew near her mother came running towards us. Crying, she dropped to her knees; she was hugging and slobbering all over Sylvia,

'Thank God you are safe, my baby; where have you been? We have been so worried about you.'

I could not understand what all the fuss was about. Sylvia's father was filled with rage.

'I might have known you would be with her,' he said, pointing his finger towards me 'How many times Sylvia, have I told you to stay away from that family?' He came towards me shouting and pointing at me still. 'You stay away from us! Don't you dare go carting Sylvia off again. Do you understand? Do you hear what I am saying – you and your family stay away from us? None of you are any good.'

I recoiled, not daring to say a word. He guided his sobbing wife and daughter up the pathway. I heard him saying to Sylvia, 'Your mother has been out of her mind with worry and she even went to the church to pray for your safe return.'

When I went indoors Mum was studying a knitting pattern and Dad was listening to the wireless; they had not even missed me. I was relieved Mr Shepherd did not complain to Dad otherwise I would have had a wallop around the head for leading Sylvia astray even though it was her idea in the first place to go exploring. Dad was quite fond of whacking me round the head when I had done something wrong. If I was sitting by the fireplace when I got a whack, my head would bang against the iron mantelpiece and I would end up having a bad headache. Dad sometimes threatened to get his belt out to me, although he never did; he only threatened it to frighten me, but his hands were big and hard enough to do me some damage. Mum would often stand between Dad and me to stop him lashing out and she took the hits quite a few times. When I was in tears Mum would give me a cup of warm milk with bread and sugar in it to soothe me.

In bed at night, I listened to Mum's and Aunty Ann's hushed voices from the other side of the screen. Aunty Ann had split up from her husband. I don't know the details only that Uncle Len had left her and was fighting for custody of the three children, Rodney, Clifford and Marion, stating that Aunty Ann was an unfit mother. He won custody in the end.

Ann must have been distraught when he was given the children but she never showed it. Not long after this Ann met a Welshman named Tony and as the fight for the children seemed to be a lost cause Aunty Ann decided to cut her losses and move to Manchester to live with him. After a few months Ann persuaded Billy to join her as she had told him he could end up like George and be forever at the beck and call of the Old Girl. I remember there was a big row and Nan accused Ann of trying to entice Billy away. Anyway Billy did decide to join Ann and live in Manchester. I was so pleased and hoped he would never come back.

May 1951 was the year the Festival of Britain was opened in Battersea, London, to mark the centenary of the Great Exhibition of 1851. I cannot remember a great deal of what was there apart from a beam of light against the night sky which you could stand under. Mum and we children queued up behind portable railings in the cold and rain, until it was after six o'clock as Mum said it would be cheaper to get in after six. She told us kids to make a run for it when the man let us in, then he would not know how many of us there were and some of us could get in without paying. The next day Mum insisted we do it all over again as she reasoned the Exhibition would not be held again for a hundred years and she wanted us to always remember it. All I can remember is that it was cold, wet and miserable.

Chapter 11

The following year I sat my 11-plus, on the sixth of February, the day King George VI died. Needless to say, I failed the exam. The King had died when his daughter, Princess Elizabeth, was on tour in Kenya. She did not know she had become Queen Elizabeth II until a few days later, as news travelled slowly in those days. After her husband, Prince Philip, broke the news to her, she flew home to join the rest of her family in mourning. Awful dull music was played on the wireless every day out of respect for the Royal Family, which was enough to make everybody miserable. Nan took me to Windsor on the day the King was to be buried in the castle. The shop windows had portraits of the king displayed on wooden easels and surrounded by purple satin material. Nan pushed me to the front of the people standing waiting by the curb side so that I would be able to see the procession. The crowds lined the streets solemnly; it was eerily quiet as the funeral cortege passed by. It was a gloomy, dull day and a lot of the people wore black armbands as was the custom then when someone had died.

The mood of the people was still very depressed for the rest of the year and well into the next, as there was one national disaster after another – plane and train crashes, freak floods in Devon and Canvey Island, which killed hundreds of people, and then in the winter came the thick poisonous pea soup fog over London that indirectly killed thousands more people and brought the city almost to a standstill..

But life for our family was just the same as usual – it was one long struggle to get by. One day George was upset as he had been out walking along the street looking for dog ends and one pair of his trousers had fallen down as the string holding them up came undone. The kids in the street saw this happen and were laughing and prancing around him calling him names. George pulled up his trousers and fiddled with the string that held them up, but the kids did not stop jeering so he began shouting and waving his arms in the air saying that everyone was 'fucking useless imbeciles' and 'King Canute couldn't even hold the tide back' I don't know what King Canute had to do with anything. George eventually came indoors and hurried along the passage into the scullery. My brother Norman entered the scullery and startled George as he was getting a drink of water at the sink. George turned round picked up a plate and threw it at Norman, catching him on the side of his head and making it bleed. Norman screamed blue murder and George screamed at him to get out of his way and to leave him alone. Dad, on hearing the commotion, rushed in and punched George in the face. George staggered backwards, the back door flew open and he stumbled out. Dad locked him out in the garden so George picked up a garden chair and bashed it through the window. Mum came rushing in, shouting at Dad for being so stupid, shutting George out when he was in such a state. Mum opened the back door for George to come in, and he then did a runner up the stairs to hide. Mum tried to calm the situation down and told Dad about the kids in the street winding George up and he could not help the way he was and 'Besides,' she added, comforting Norman, 'he only has a small cut and I don't want any more bloody trouble.'

The trouble did not stop, though, as Nan had another big

row with the Shepherds and with the sisters, Armhole and Eagle Beak. This was over George shouting and swearing at people yet again and they complained about the mountain of rubbish stacked high in the back garden which they said encouraged rats. Mr Shepherd had had enough so he started up a petition for the neighbours to sign and then to be taken to the court to apply for an eviction order to get Nan and George out. Many of the neighbours had signed and it was presented in court and accepted, so Nan and George were ordered to leave. I was at school the day Nan and George were evicted. A few people had gathered around watching as everything she owned was dumped onto the front garden and pavement. Nan cried, not knowing what to do or where to go. She arranged for her belongings to be put into storage and important papers and letters went into the left luggage boxes at King's Cross Station. Nan and George walked the streets and slept under the bridges on the Thames Embankment. Many of the neighbours said it was a shame what had happened and told Mum that they had not signed the petition, but Mum told us they were lying and for us not to trust anyone; if they were to ask where Nan and George had gone, we were to tell them we didn't know. The story was in the local newspapers and Mum felt humiliated and shame that her mother and brother were thrown out onto the streets. She also worried about who would be moving in upstairs now they were gone.

I just hoped the Shepherds and the two sisters now felt ashamed of themselves for starting all this by getting an old woman and a mentally ill man evicted, but I don't suppose they did.

Dad was warned by a man at the rent office that Nan and George were never to enter 17 St John's Avenue again; if they were to enter the house then our family would be evicted, too. Dad agreed to this and then asked if he could rent the flat upstairs himself for his growing family. Dad worked hard clearing the rest of the rubbish left upstairs and in the back garden. He had a massive bonfire in the back garden to get rid of most of it and the dustbin men grumbled when they took the rest of it. Dad rewired the electrics and every day after work and at weekends he painted and decorated the flat. He was quiet one evening when he came downstairs and Mum asked him what the matter was; he replied that, whilst he was up a ladder putting up a roll of wallpaper, he had seen a ghost glide across the room and vanish through the wall. This was the first of many sightings and disturbances witnessed by different people, but I never saw a ghost in the house. Dad asked a neighbour, who had lived in the road since before our family had moved in, about this matter and the neighbour said the previous tenants had told him the same thing – the flat upstairs was haunted and they had seen the same ghost and had moved out because they were frightened.

That same year that Nan had left was a big turning point in my life as Mum and Dad had to decide what senior school I should join in the September. They asked what school I wanted to go to and I replied I wanted to go to a school where people would not know about Nan and George. I said there was a girls' school I had heard about which was a few miles away and I would like to go there. So that was settled – Mum and Dad put me down for Dudden Hill Girls Secondary Modern School, even though they moaned a little about paying the bus fare every day.

My brothers and I were always trying to think of ways to raise money. I wanted to have my ears pierced, Norman wanted a set of toy metal building pieces, and Ken wanted to buy toy cars as he could only play with our shoes, pretending they were cars. David was still too young to earn pocket money. Ken ran errands for an old lady, Mrs Chapman, who lived a few doors up from us. Norman and I looked forward to Cup Final day every year, not that we were interested in football, but because all the children in the district would line the main roads leading to Wembley Stadium. When the coaches passed the kids would all scream 'Throw out yer moldies!' and the people on the coaches would throw out handfuls of pennies, florins, sixpences and, if you were in luck, half a crown. The Scotsmen were very generous but the English were stingy, so we did not shout ourselves hoarse at their coaches. We scrambled into the road, pushing and shoving each other to retrieve the coins. It was a wonder that we didn't get killed in the stampede. This was an excellent way for us to get some money. I was chuffed when I gave Mum a half-crown that I had almost come to blows over with a kid in the rush to pick it up. Mum almost cried when I gave it to her as she did not have any money that day. She went to the butcher's to buy a marrowbone and cooked it with vegetables and dumplings.

One day I was out trying to earn money by collecting newspapers. I was knocking on front doors asking people for their old papers. I then piled them onto the pushchair and wheeled them to the paper and rag yard to sell. I walked for miles as the more paper I collected the more money I earned. I was pushing a heavy load of these newspapers when I felt sticky down below. I went home to go to the toilet and I was bleeding. I did not know what was wrong or what to do; I had never been told about the facts of life. I felt panicky and thought I was going to die because it had to be something to do with what Billy had done to me. I put a piece of old rag into my knickers and was relieved when the bleeding stopped after a day or so and I had not died. A few weeks later I began to bleed again, so, crying, I told my mum that I was going to die as I was bleeding to death. Mum said she would talk to me later when it was quiet. I was still sleeping in the living room as Dad had not finished decorating upstairs yet. Mum sat on the end of the bed with a folded-up baby's napkin, and said: 'Put this in your knickers until I can buy the proper thing for you to wear.' Puzzled, I took the nappy from her as she added, 'It is bad blood, Rosie, and bad blood has to come out.'

With that, she left without saying another word. I was mortified. So that was it then, I thought, that was the proof. I was wicked and had bad blood in me. I quietly cried myself to sleep.

Chapter 12

That same summer, as I turned twelve, I was not only apprehensive about starting senior school but I was worried about the changes in my body. However, I tried to put it to the back of my mind and to just enjoy the summer break. My brothers and I met up with the Shepherd girls and we went to the local park to see the Willesden Show. This was always a big event every year. We watched the parade of jugglers, stilt walkers, decorated horse and carts, people in fancy dress, marching bands, dancing girls, and finally the Carnival Court as they paraded pass, ending up in Roundwood Park. This was the one day of the year when there would be a charge to enter the park. We children were really annoyed that we would have to pay to get into the park, so we didn't pay; we went unseen along the wooden fence until we came to a part that was hidden by bushes, where we broke the wood panels and climbed through. It was such an exciting and marvellous, colourful event that almost the whole neighbourhood looked forward to going there. In the showground there were giant marquees where flower and vegetable competitions were held along with 'The Bonnie Baby' and the 'Fancy Dress Competition' and outside of the tents the Punch and Judy show. Loud music could be heard for miles around. There were colourful painted wagons and displays;

gypsy women selling toffee apples that were so hard they could almost break your jaw; stallholders beckoning to us to roll a penny or win a coconut on the coconut shy... It was all amazing to us and we loved it. Besides the dodgems, big wheel, carousels and other fast-moving contraptions to ride on, there were also the side shows where one could pay to see anything from a bearded lady to a two-headed man. We sneaked in to see the 'only man in the world that could balance on one finger'. Before I had left to go to the fair, Mum had given me a black satin, fringed skirt to play 'dressing up' in. The fringe on the skirt was about eight inches long – it must have once been a lampshade – but nevertheless I liked it as I was fond of playing 'dressing up'. I wore the skirt to the Willesden Show, as I thought lots of people would be in fancy dress and I would look as if I belonged there and the park-keeper would not sling me out. But anyone could see I was still a scruffy kid – with or without the skirt on.

I think the post-war years failed young people by pretending that the world had now got rid of the evil that had threatened every one of us. We were told Britain was now a nice, peaceful, safe place to live. Was it? I don't think so! Little did youngsters like me appreciate that the danger was always around us every day in the form of men wearing the cloak of respectability. At the age of twelve years old, despite Billy, I was still very naïve. That day in the park I had lost my brothers and the Shepherd girls in the fairground and so I wandered off into the crowd. I had a penny which I rolled down on the Roll-a-Penny stall, it landed on the threepence square without touching the lines and the stall holder threw me three pennies which I promptly rolled down again and lost. I turned round to see that a smart-looking man, dressed in a grey suit, was watching me.

'Oh bad luck!' he said in a pleasant voice. 'Here, roll this penny for me – it may bring you luck.'

I took the penny he handed me, rolled and lost.

'Sorry,' I said to him and went to move off.

'You look good in that skirt. I bet it flares out when you twist around.'

I said, 'Yes it does,' and walked on.

He followed. 'I'll give you another penny if you twist round for me.'

I laughed and twisted around, sending the fringing flying upwards. The man bent his head; the dirty sod was looking at my knickers. He put a penny in my palm. 'If you put your hand in my pocket, you will find a sixpence.' I knew there would be much more than a sixpence in there so I threw the penny at him and ran off.

I soon forgot all about this man, and I met up with a fair-haired girl named Joyce. I knew Joyce vaguely from junior school and she told me she was going to attend Dudden Hill Girls' School the same as I was and she said we could be friends when we started. I was really pleased to find a new friend and she did not mention Nan or George at all. Joyce and I stayed in the park until it was dark as we wanted to watch the man who was going to dive from a great height into a few inches of water that would be covered with oil and set alight. The crowd gasped as the oil was lit and, amid much excitement, the man dived in. The fairground people then went around with a box to collect money. All of a sudden there was a heavy cloudburst. Joyce and I ran to stand under a tree; we were soaked and the black fringing on my skirt looked a sight clinging to my legs. Joyce lived just outside the park, in the rough Curzon Crescent estate, so we decided to make a run for it.

Joyce's mum opened the door to what must have looked like two drowned rats. She kindly made us a hot drink as we dried ourselves off with a large towel. Although we were happy and laughing sipping our cocoa, I was becoming worried as it was getting late and Dad had been now laying down the law as to what time I had to be back home each evening. If I was late, he would whack my head as I walked passed him to the front door. Joyce's dad had a van so he took me home and explained to my mum what had happened. I returned the next day to see Joyce and her mum and to thank them. I told Joyce I had saved enough money to have my ears pierced. She said she knew a shop where I could have it done, so we both set off to walk about three or four miles to a shop in the Harrow Road. I had sleeper earrings put in and given a bottle of spirits to dab on my ears every day. When we arrived back at her home I fainted on the doorstep.

The following day the Shepherd girls were very envious of my pierced ears. I pretended that it was no big deal and I could have pieced my ears myself.

'Could you really?' they said.

'Course I could. I could even do yours if you wanted me to,' I boasted.

They looked doubtful. 'All right, do our ears then.'

'All right I will,' I replied, 'but I will have to wait until it's darker in case your dad sees us or he will give you a good hiding if he sees you with me.'

I was hoping that they would be too afraid of their dad to go through with it. But they were eager to have their ears pierced and said they would meet me later. There was no going back now; I would have to go along with it. That evening I met the girls under the old lamp-post that was our usual meeting place. I had come prepared with a cork, a needle and cotton and Vaseline.

Sylvia was first. I pretended I knew what I was doing, I told her that she would have to be quiet and grit her teeth when I put the needle in. I smoothed on the Vaseline and held the cork behind her ear. The needle went halfway in and she yelped. 'Shut up!' I said and quickly shoved the needle right through and pulled the cotton out of the back of her earlobe, then unthreaded the needle and tied a knot in the thread. I then did the other ear and told her knowingly that she must turn the thread every day. I then did her sister Pauline's ears. Brenda decided that she did not want hers done. I made them swear that they must never tell their dad who had pierced their ears or I would give them a hiding. I was relieved they did not tell him it was me that had pierced their ears. It is a wonder that the girls did not get blood poisoning. The girls were really pleased, though, as their mother bought them a pair of gold earrings each to use instead of the cotton.

On a sunny day that summer, Mum asked me to take the boys out. I went with them to Willesden Junction and we stood on the bridge to watch the steam trains pass and to write their numbers down in an exercise book. I did not see the point of collecting train numbers, but it kept us occupied for a while. When the trains passed beneath the bridge the boys jumped for joy when the train driver waved at them, and then when the smoke billowed out from the chimney it made us cough and splutter but we went home happy and with sooty faces.

The summer was finally over and I was going to start the new school. I felt grown up and proud carrying my little blue case holding my new fountain pen, bottle of ink, rubber and ruler. Mum bought me a navy-blue skirt and white blouse and a dark-blue cardigan. I went by trolleybus from Harlesden to Willesden High Road, and then walked the rest of the way to the school. Joyce was in a different class to me, but we met up in the playground. I soon made friends with other girls, including the girl I sat next to, Sheila Thomas; we stayed friends throughout our time at Dudden Hill.

The autumn was very cold. In December there came the dense fog that brought the city to a standstill. The damp, noxious fumes indirectly killed some 4,000 people,

Mum was really badly affected by the fog and her cough was getting her down. Mum was also pregnant again, but she still struggled to the shops to buy food for us with the little money she had. Dad had also been unwell but had to go back to work after he had a few days off; he had to return to work even though he was still unwell, otherwise there would be no money to feed us at all. We children also went down with colds and snotty noses. Christmas was looming. We never had meat or poultry at Christmas time as meat was still on ration. We had potatoes and greens or cauliflower together with the spotted dick pudding that Mum made with flour, currants and suet.

At school I did not like morning assembly but before the term broke up for the Christmas holiday I did enjoy the carols we sang, even if I thought some of them were too long. I also liked the Salvation Army band that played in the High Street; sometimes they would play their instruments in the freezing fog. The sound of the big bass drum and the trumpets would vibrate right through me but I always stood around watching them as I enjoyed listening to the carols.

On Christmas Eve Mum trudged off to the shops, with us children in tow, just before closing time as usual. She would ask for the cheap leftover bread and stale cakes in the baker's, then went to the grocer's for the cracked eggs and two ounces of butter, which the shopkeeper would take out of the butter tub with his wooden specula, pat into a square, then wrap in greaseproof paper. Finally it was to the green-grocer's for the old 'specks' and a Christmas tree which Mum would buy for next to nothing. I didn't like it if Mum stopped to talk with a woman named Mrs Baggers, as it was difficult to get away from her and we children became restless in the cold and they would chat for ages. Mrs Baggers lived in the next road to us; she always wore a long skirt and black coat and a feathered hat on her head. She reminded me of a mummy duck waddling along with her shopping on a small pushchair. She always knew everything that was going on in the neighbourhood, which she would pass on to everybody she met.

Mum had saved the silver milk bottle tops for us to make

decorations for the tree, and we children carefully threaded them on to cotton. I made a paper dress and silver paper wings for a small doll to go on top of the tree. My brothers made glue with flour and water and stuck strips of coloured paper together, and then we all helped to hang the paper chains up across the ceiling.

I was still sleeping on the bed in the living room and it was so cold I had a mountain of old coats on the bed. My brothers and I sat on the bed and mum gave us a cup with a spoonful of cocoa powder in. Mum said that if we beat it long enough it would turn into chocolate. We beat and beat the cocoa with a fork, and when we became too tired to beat any more and the cocoa had not turned into chocolate, Mum said, 'Oh well, never mind,' and poured hot water on it for a nice warm drink before we went to sleep. I think Mum did this to keep us quiet for a while. I looked forward to Christmas morning even though I knew I would be receiving a magic painting book again. The book was called a magic painting book as when you wet the page the picture would, as if by magic, become coloured. We hung our socks up and Christmas morning we found an apple and orange in them that was only slightly bruised. Mum hung up a pillowcase and jokingly said Father Christmas might take pity on her and fill it with lots of nice things. We fell about laughing when Mum found her pillow case was full and then when she dug into it she found an old saucepan lid, a dented frying pan, a rotten potato, an old stiff paintbrush, an onion and a broom head. We kids thought this was hilarious as she pretended to cry with an exaggeratedly loud 'boohoo'. It made me realize how lucky I was to receive a magic paint book.

After Christmas I returned to school, and the teacher asked us all to write in our exercise book what we had had for Christmas. This was a chance to let my imagination run away with me and I described all the presents I would have liked to have received, like a 'walkie-talkie' doll that could say 'Mama' when tipped sideways and which opened and closed her eyes and also moved her legs backwards and forwards as if she could walk.

In the January of 1953 I had a new baby sister; Mum and Dad named her Joyce Violet.

Yes, these were harsh times, but the love my mother had for us all always shone through the bleakness of the dark days.

Chapter 13

When I think back to my early life I can only view it as being not really about me but another person, a child that existed long ago in another life, as if in a black-and-white picture. I do not see my early life in colour at all, though it does remind me of an old film I once saw which started off in black and white, but which then, about ten minutes in, changed into colour. I was now twelve years old and my life seemed to be changing gradually into faint colours with the birth of my baby sister, Joyce, and with Billy now being miles away from me in Manchester. I sometimes hurried home from school just to see Joyce. She would smile and wave her arms with excitement when she saw me and I played and nursed her for hours. I did not feel quite alone now as I had her to love and make a fuss of. I was growing up very fast; I was bigger and much more mature than other girls of my age and a lot of people mistook me for being a lot older than I was.

Mum and Dad now rented upstairs and I was given a bedroom to myself at the back of the house. I even had a dressing table, wardrobe and a chest of drawers. I was beginning to feel a lot happier; the only complaint I had was that the bedroom was so cold. The covers on the bed were still made up of all the old coats and a satin eiderdown that never stayed on the bed at the night as it was silky. The downstairs living room was still the same, an untidy mess. The upstairs room at the front of the house, with the gas lamps above the mantelpiece, was now the 'best room', which would only be used if someone came to visit. The front room downstairs was the bedroom for Mum and Dad. The boys slept upstairs where they had more room to play. Little David was not a happy child; he had a lot of trouble with his eyes. David had what was called a lazy eye, so he wore a sticky plaster on one of the lenses of his glasses, over the good eye, to try to strengthen the weak one; he would cry a lot, which seemed to get on everyone's nerves. I don't think it helped him having two older brothers who overshadowed him and a baby sister needing a lot of attention.

After the depressing winter, the excitement of the forth-coming Coronation was dominating the newspapers. The talk in our house was mainly about John Christie, who was wanted in connection with the murder of three women who had been found boarded up behind the wallpaper in a house he had lived in. Christie had given evidence in a murder trial that had led to the hanging of his lodger, Timothy Evans, for killing his wife and daughter. I was playing with Joyce whilst Mum was doing the ironing. There were no wall sockets in the house, so the iron had to be plugged into a brown plastic, two way plug in the ceiling light. The light bulb and shade swung back and forth with every swing of the iron over the clothes; it was a wonder that the bulb did not fall out.

'He lived near Ann you know,' Mum said, ironing the front of the clothes only, as she said it was a waste of time doing where no one could see. 'And we have walked past his road, Rillington Place, in Notting Hill Gate, so many times. To think there were bodies plastered behind the walls. We could even have passed Christie, a murderer, in the street. It doesn't bear thinking about.'

Dad was reading his newspaper at the table. 'Have you nearly finished, Nell?' he asked irritably; Dad always referred to Mum as Nell. 'That light swinging back and forth is making my eyes bad. Anyway, I heard he used to work at The Crypto so I may have even worked with him.'

Mum gave a shiver as she quickly rubbed the iron over the remaining items.

'Well, you be careful in case he is lingering about near here.'

Christie was finally caught, and sentenced to death. Years later Timothy Evens was pardoned, but of course it was too late for that poor soul.

We children had something to be joyful about though, as sweets had come off of the ration that spring and Norman, Kenny and I joined the other kids in the long queue outside the sweet shop waiting for opening time. When the shop finally opened we all surged in. You would have thought the shops were only ever going to sell sweets for this one day only. Dad was now working seven days a week and he was giving us pocket money; I received six pence per week, which I spent all in one go on that day. I bought a sherbet fountain, a gobstopper, two ounces of Sharps toffees and a penny chocolate.

The excitement of the forthcoming Coronation on 2 June 1953 was dominating the country and preparations were in full swing. In the schools the children were preparing for the Coronation by learning the history of the kings and queens of England, especially about Queen Elizabeth I and Henry VIII. I collected cuttings from newspapers and magazines to cut out and stick in a scrapbook. The shops were full of memorabilia and all the children in the country were given a Coronation cup, saucer and plate and a five shilling crown in a clear plastic case. Mum bought Norman a toy Matchbox replica of the Golden Coach, which would carry the Queen to Westminster Abbey for her to take the Coronation Oath and to be crowned by Dr Fisher, the Archbishop of Canterbury. We were also excited as Dad bought a 9-inch television with the extra money he was earning, though he said we were not allowed to touch it, insisting he would be the only one to turn it off or on. But Mum turned it on anyway when Dad was at work and she turned it off just before he was due home. We kids thought it was wonderful to have a television and we would sit and watch the test card for what seemed to be ages before the music started up to indicate the programme was about to start.

Weeks before the Coronation, Mum took a chair outside the house to climb on and we all helped her decorate the outside of the house. We put up banners of red, white and blue, a Union Jack attached to a broom handle, Coronation posters of the Queen and even memorabilia cups and plates inside the windowsill. When the great day came we huddled in front of the television to watch the whole thing on our small screen. Brother Norman held the indoor aerial up so as to receive the best signal and we had to jump up and down on the floor when the screen flickered or broke down. Mum said it was such a shame that it was a rainy day as hundreds of people had slept on the pavements overnight on the procession route. That same week as the Coronation, Mount Everest was conquered by the expedition led by Colonel John Hunt, so the whole country was in a joyful mood.

In the six-week summer break Dad had a week off work and he took me to Newcastle to visit his parents. Mum bought me two new dresses and, for the first time ever, a new pair of shoes. I was so excited having these new brown leather shoes that I put them on and walked up and down our road, glancing at people as they passed to see if they noticed my shoes. When I got back Dad gave me a clout around the ear as I had worn the backs down. After the long journey to Newcastle by train, I was so pleased to meet up with my grandparents, cousins and uncle and aunts. I had so missed them and that wonderful friendly Geordie accent. We all visited the coast, including South Shields and Scarborough where I got lost and had to tell a fisherman tending his nets that I could not find my dad and family. He asked me where I was staying and I could not remember the address in Gateshead so he said to stay there beside the boat until my dad found me. I did not worry as the fisherman brought me an ice cream and I sat licking it whilst sitting on the sand until Dad came along. I remember this well as it was my thirteenth birthday.

When we arrived back in London and I got fed up not knowing what to do with myself as most of my friends from school did not live near me, I went for long walks on my own, even in the rain. I walked along the High Street and looked in the shop windows at all the lovely things you could buy if only you had lots of money. On these walks there would always be someone to meet up with to have a chat to. Mum was still breastfeeding Joyce and every Friday evening she would take all us children to the cinema whilst Dad was in the Working Men's Club. I cringed when Mum sat breastfeeding Joyce to keep her quiet during the film. After a while I told Mum I no longer wanted to go with her. She was not pleased about this, but I insisted I would not go by throwing a tantrum until she agreed I could stay at home. As I was too afraid to be in the darkened house by myself, I would sit in the porch until either Mum or Dad came home.

Across the road from our house, upstairs to the Cobbs, lived a young man named Bob, who lived with his mother. Bob had TB and was too ill to go out on his own, but he enjoyed taking photographs with his large square wooden camera. He developed his own photos from the glass negatives in a blacked-out room. He and his mother, Mrs Pullen, were nice people and Bob would sometimes venture across the road to our front garden to take photos of us children. One day, in early springtime, Mrs Pullen asked Mum if I would like to go to Margate with Bob, his brother and her. I could not believe that of all the children in our road they chose me to go with them. Bob's brother had a car; it felt very strange to travel in this little car as I had never been in one before and I did not even know of anyone who owned a car. I was mesmerized by the open roads and fields and the way Bob's brother started the engine up with a starting handle he twisted round and round at the front of the car. There were little yellow plastic indicators that lifted up, to use when turning corners. I felt very privileged to be with them on this day out and they did not mention Nan and George at all. We had a lovely picnic of sandwiches and lemonade on the beach and I walked along the jetty looking for crabs and fish. I remember this beautiful day well and the colours of my life seemed to begin then. Bob took lots of photos of me, which I treasured. After this day I would sometimes go to see him and he would take photos of me with baby Joyce. Bob restored my confidence in men as he was such a kind person and always had time to talk with me, despite him being so very ill, painfully thin and breathless. Bob died a few years later of this dreadful disease, but I never forgot his and his mother's kindness.

Chapter 14

I had been doing fine at my school work and had made a lot of new friends. My best friend now was a girl in my class named Sheila Thomas and we would meet up after school outside her house, which was only about a mile away. I had to make sure I was not home late, because, now I was growing up fast and blossoming out, Dad was now getting very strict about what time I came home in the evenings. After I came home from school I'd have a slice of bread and then go straight out. I hated being indoors with my brothers as I would end up having a fight with them as I thought they were so annoying and then I would get into trouble. If I were to come home even a few minutes late, Dad would give me a good hiding. But I know he and Mum were only worried about me.

Back at school in the September after my thirteenth birthday, I was put in a midstream class with the worst form teacher in the school, Mrs Maxiner. She had a reputation as being a nasty, bossy bully who terrified all the girls. She took a great delight in slapping pupils' arms with a wide plastic ruler; she viciously smacked their arms over and over again and only stopped when she herself was out of breath. Mrs Maxiner wore big plastic owl glasses over her ice-cold, hateful eyes. The poor girls who were subject to her anger, over what could have been the least little thing they had done, ended up sobbing so much they would be hyperventilating. The other girls witnessing this punishment would be close to tears. We all hated and feared her vicious temper. As far as I was concerned, if she hated us girls so much she should never have been a teacher in the first place. One day I was whispering to another girl in our class, and Mrs Maxiner called me out to the front then she smacked my arm so much the ruler flipped from her hand. My arm was red and bruised and I sobbed with the pain and humiliation and, like the other girls who were subjected to this assault, I could hardly catch my breath. As usual no child would ever tell their parents what had happened in school, including me. When I went home that day I rolled down my sleeve so my mum did not see the bruising, not that she would have done anything if she had seen it. So as well as being fearful of my father at home, I was also fearful of the bully teacher at school. It was at this time I began to have nightmares. Dad would put his head around the bedroom door to make sure I was asleep before turning the light off. The minute the light went out I would jump out of bed screaming and banging the door, shouting for someone to let me out (though the door wasn't locked). I would then fall to the floor covering my ears and crying uncontrollably. Mum would come running to me and she and Dad would put me back into bed. This happened at least once or twice a week and Mum did not know what to do about it, so they did nothing and hoped I would grow out of it in time.

Being thirteen and a moody teenager now, one evening I was in such a bad mood and said 'Oh damn' after one of my brothers had annoyed me. Dad hit me so hard my teeth went through my lip and I ended up with a face that was bruised and swollen. The next morning it looked worse than ever and my mum said I should have the day off school. I was defiant and shouted at Mum, saying I was going to go to school and, if anyone asked me who did it, I would tell them it was my father. The strange thing is that not one teacher asked me what had happened. I think in those days teachers turned a blind eye to most things.

Dad said I now had to be home by eight o'clock in the evenings. If I was late, I would be in a lot of trouble with him. I did not own a watch so I would have to ask a passer-by what the time was. Dad had already given me a wallop the evening before for being late home by just ten minutes and I was late again after I had been hanging out with my friend Sheila outside her house. I had asked a policeman who was passing by what the time was, and he said eight thirty. 'Oh no!' I said, really worried now as I was going to be late back. The policeman could see I was troubled so I told him my dad would be giving me a telling off for being late. He said he would see me home. Dad was on the doorstep waiting.

'Oh yes, what's all this about then?' said Dad.

'Your daughter was afraid to come home as she was late so I saw her home.'

Dad was furious. 'Get in now!' he spat.

I ran in and upstairs, passing Mum on the way, and slammed the door.

Dad shouted up the stairs that that was it – I was now not allowed out for a week.

I felt like a prisoner having to stay in every evening for the next week and I was so sulky and moody. My brothers annoyed me so much I ended up arguing all the time with them. Mum said I was to do more around the house and I argued that the house was a tip and I would not be able to do it all and it was unfair to ask me to. Next evening Mum was waiting for me when I came home from school and directed me to the scullery, where there was a bowl of water ready for me to do the washing up. I washed the dishes and saucepans and banged them about in protest. Mum got so fed up with me and my moody ways, she was glad when I could go out again. The following week I went to hang out with a small gang of school friends outside Sheila's house again. I did not realize it was getting so late and when I found out the time I panicked. I knew I would be in trouble again and it would take me about twenty minutes to get home. I was running as fast as I could up the road – it was a dark November evening. Dad was waiting on the doorstep. My heart was thumping with fear as I knew he would be angry and I knew he would hit me all the way up the pathway and into the house. I felt unwell, my legs were shaking, and, by breathing in the smog of the past few days, I now had a bad cough as well. On top of this I also had bad stomach cramps. I could feel a stitch in my side so I stopped running. What was the use? I thought. He would hit me anyway now. I tried to catch my breath and knew I just could not face Dad that evening, so I turned and fled, not knowing where I was going to go. I walked aimlessly until eventually I came to the park. I found a loose slat to force my way through, then made my way in the dark to the park-keeper's hut – it wasn't locked. I spent the night in there afraid and freezing cold, sitting on a deckchair. I was frightened but not as frightened as I was to face Dad. When it was just getting light I ventured home, hoping my father would be at work. He was. I told Mum that I had stayed with a girl named Maureen from the next road to ours and I had no way of letting her know I would be staying there. Very few people had phones in those days so I mistakenly thought I could get away with it. When my father came home from work he went to see Maureen's mother and was told I had not been there. It was Guy Fawkes Day and when Dad got back he did not say a word, other than for me to get my coat and come with him. We passed huge burning bonfires on the rubble of the bomb sites, and there were people feeding the fires with old furniture and rubbish, whilst the kids were having fun with sparklers and fireworks. The air was filled with the smell of burning as Dad marched me to the police station. I did not want to go in, so Dad got hold of me and dragged me in. He spoke to someone on the desk, and then I was told to follow a tall broad man into a small room. Dad shoved me to go in, but he remained outside. The man was not in a uniform. He asked me to sit down, and a police-woman joined us. They asked me where I had spent the previous night.

'Nowhere,' I answered defiantly.

'You had to be somewhere, so where was you?' said the man.

I did not answer. The policewoman said the sooner I answered the questions the sooner I could leave.

'I stayed in a shop doorway,' I lied.

'What shop doorway?'

'One in the High Road; I forget what the shop was called.'

'Were you with a boy?'

I looked surprised. 'No I was not'

They both stared at me waiting for me to say more, but I didn't.

The policewoman got up and dragged me, struggling, along a corridor, to a police cell and slammed it shut. The cell smelt of wee and disinfectant. I was sobbing uncontrollably, banging my fists against the door, just like I had done so in my bedroom when Dad had turned the light out. I felt panicky and as if I was unable to breathe. It was stifling and I was shut in with no escape. I was left in the cell for hours and every now and again someone pulled back the slat to take a look at me and then slammed it shut again. I was petrified and shaking uncontrollably. When I could cry no longer; I sat on the hard wooden bench shaking and tried to occupy myself by studying the disgusting graffiti on the walls. After a few hours the door was unlocked by the policewoman and without a word from my father he took me home and he told me to go straight to bed.

Next day I could hear Mum and Dad having a big row about

what was going to happen to me. When I ventured downstairs they both screamed at me. I covered my ears, as they both shouted that I was out of control and that I was going to be put away into a children's home for 'being in need of care and protection'. Dad said they could not cope with me anymore as I did not take a blind bit of notice of what they said to me. Later, as I sat on my bed, I could hear Mum crying and shouting again at my dad. They called for me to come downstairs when a policewoman arrived to take me to the court for the order to put me away. She was a tall, skinny woman who reminded me of the shape of a new moon. She spoke to my parents in a quiet voice before turning to me and said in a stern voice, 'Your mother and father have decided that they do not want you to go into care.' She let me take this in before adding, 'Well, what have you to say to your mother and father?'

I said nothing.

'I asked you what you have to say to your parents – or do you want them to change their mind and send you away?'

I lowered my head. 'Sorry,' I whispered.

'Louder!' the moon woman said.

'Sorry,' I repeated, louder this time.

'Right,' the policewoman said, turning to my mother 'She will need to go to the doctor to be examined before we can close this matter.'

'Get indoors and go to your bedroom,' said my father angrily, 'and you can stay there until I say you can come out.'

That afternoon mum took me to the doctor's. I couldn't remember going to the doctor's before and I was shaking with fear whilst we sat in the waiting room. Other people waiting to see the doctor were silently staring at me. Eventually we were asked to go in by the receptionist. Mum handed the doctor a form from the police station. He studied it, looked at me above his glasses and then he asked me to take off my underwear and get onto the couch and turn on my side. There was not a screen so Mum sat watching. The doctor lifted my leg up and his finger prodded me.

'All right, you can get down now and put your things back on.'

I welled up and the tears started to flow. I sniffed on a piece of rag from my sleeve. I felt degraded and humiliated.

The doctor nodded to my mother. 'She's all right.' He wrote something down on a sheet of paper and gave it to her. 'Give this to the officer in charge at the station'

Mum nagged me on the way home. 'This is entirely your own fault, Rosie; you don't do a thing you are told. Fancy you staying in a shop doorway all night. You are nothing but trouble and a worry to us. You are a bad girl and I don't know what is to become of you.'

That evening in my bedroom I broke down again and sobbed for ages. My face was hot and puffed, my head ached, and I was tired and weary. I hated my father and vowed that I would never forgive him for putting me through all of this. I blamed Dad for everything. If he had not been waiting on the doorstep to give me a good hiding for being late home that night, I would never have run away. I felt so sorry for myself and wanted to be grown up so I would be able to do what I wanted to.

Chapter 15

The following few days I tried to stay out of the way when my father was in the house. Mum said Dad had insisted again that I was not to go out for at least a week as a punishment and I was to do all the washing up each evening. As we did not have running hot water, this meant having to boil up a kettle to pour into a chipped enamel bowl. I always made more mess than there already was as I kept spilling the water on the floor. After a few days Mum relented, and said I could go out but to be back at home before Dad came in round about seven o'clock, so I just hung out with the kids in our road until just before Dad was due home.

At night I sometimes dreaded going to sleep just in case the nightmare returned of me being swept away after a train goes into a river. After this nightmare I would always awake gasping for air, thinking I was drowning. Because of this, I tried to keep awake for as long as I could by trying to visualize what the front-page headlines would be in the next day's morning newspaper. I'd close my eyes and see the headlines so clearly. Next morning I would surprise myself when I saw the newspaper as I was almost always right. I still awoke sometimes, hammering my fists on the bedroom door.

One Saturday afternoon in the following spring, Mum was out and I was rocking Joyce in my arms. She was irritable and restless and I was trying to calm her until Mum got home. Dad came into the room, wearing his braces over his rolled-up greyish shirt and puffing on a Woodbine. He barely looked at me, as nowadays we had nothing much to say to each other.

Dad picked up his newspaper and I could see he was getting annoyed.

He said sharply, 'Keep her quiet!'

'That's what I am trying to do,' I snapped back.

'Don't you get lippy with me.' He took a step forward; I was almost as tall as him now.

'You stay away from me, do you hear?' I said defiantly, trying to hush Joyce. 'I don't care anymore what you say or do' I added, now feeling the resentment rising in me, 'and if I live to be a hundred I will never forgive you for what you put me through last November. I will tell you right now: don't you ever lay a finger on me again and don't you ever lay a finger on my sister Joyce either, because if you do you will be sorry, very sorry indeed.'

Dad went to move forward towards me again but changed his mind. He pointed his finger at me. 'You, my girl, will end up on the end of a rope one day. You are rotten, rotten to the core.'

I narrowed my eyes and I squared up to him; by now Joyce was screaming. 'You shut up and leave me alone because I hate you,' I said.

At this moment Mum rushed in, still wearing her coat and hat, and took Joyce from me. 'I am fed up with all this aggravation going on. Pack it up now, both of you. I can't stand this any longer.'

I went running to my bedroom, shocked at myself for this outburst. I could hardly believe I had said those things to Dad. Was it true what he had said? Was I really going to end up being hanged one day? I thought about Pop and Billy; it must have been my fault what had happened and now there was no hope for me. I was doomed.

Although I had been shaken by my outburst, it had some-how given me a new sense of power as I thought no matter what I did I would always be a bad person like Dad had said. I suppose my hormones were working overtime, too. I became more and more defiant and argumentative. I lashed out at my brothers, Norman and Kenny, giving them a wallop on their backs, sometimes for no reason other than just for them being there and in my way. I just could not seem to help myself, and the more rebellious I was, the unhappier I became.

I was cheeky to my mum and answered her back when she asked me to do anything. I was hateful and Mum ended up swearing at me.

'See this poker?' she said angrily one day, when she was at the end of her tether, 'It's going into the fire and you are going to get it across your face.' Mum put the poker into the fire until the steel was glowing red hot and then she chased me around the dinner table with it. Luckily, she never caught me and, even if she had, I don't think she would have hit me with the poker. It was pure frustration at not knowing how to cope with me.

Sometimes I would spend my bus fare home from school, and then the long walk home would take me about an hour. I had a choice: I could either walk home through the park or take the quicker route through a very large cemetery, but if I chose to go through the cemetery, I had to run as fast as I could so I had enough time to make it to the gate on the other side before it became too dark and the gates would be locked. If I took this route, I would hurry pass the headstones of long-dead people, the wreaths of sickly smelly flowers, and the piles of clay from the newly dug graves. I would run and run past the white stoned angels with the hollow eyes, before their shadows could catch me. Sometimes it did not seem worthwhile to take this way home and to scare myself like this.

At school I was also becoming rebellious and would get into all sorts of mischief. Mum and Dad sometimes received letters from the school asking for them to go to see the form teacher but Mum just ignored them as she said she had too much to do than to spend time going there. My parents never ever went to open days; I don't think they even knew where the school was, and that suited me fine.

One day Mrs Maxiner laid into a very timid girl with her plastic ruler. The girl was a little thing that never caused any trouble to anyone, yet she was singled out for punishment by this teacher. The poor girl almost sobbed her heart out after her lashing, and I felt so sorry for her, so next morning I crept into the classroom before anyone else came in and took the plastic ruler and hid it under Mrs Maxiner's own desk, so no one else would be subjected to this sadistic, evil cow's punishment. Mrs Maxiner made everyone turn out their desks to find it and said we would all get detention if her ruler was not returned to her by the end of the day. She did not get it back – far better we all did detention by staying an extra half-hour after school, than for her to use her ruler on us again.

Another day a few of us girls were playing along the road, during the lunch break, lifting each other's skirts up to show our knickers and running away. We thought this was funny, but it was me that had been identified by one of the teachers as she passed by in her car. Back at the school I was told to go to the head mistress's office. She asked who the other girls were that were bringing the school's reputation into disrepute. I didn't tell her. I just said they were from the Pound Lane School, which was about half a mile away. The head mistress did not believe me, so I was given three strokes of the cane on each hand as an example to other girls not to bring disgrace to the school by such bad behaviour. I did not blink an eyelid as the cane came swishing down on each hand. Afterwards I was told by the head mistress that my name would be in the punishment book for ever. 'So what?' I mumbled under my breath as I stormed out, 'I don't care!' Later I showed the girls the deep weals on my palms. They thought I was a hero.

Dad had now agreed that I could come in at nine o'clock in the evenings but the tension at home still carried on. I began attending Sunday school at the Methodist church, as Sundays were so boring and I just wanted to be out of the house. Sunday dinner was always late, so I would arrive there when the class was almost over. Before I was just about to leave the house Dad always said sarcastically to me, 'Yes, That's right go and have all your sins forgiven.' I ignored him, pulled a face and slammed the door when I left.

I asked Mum if I had been christened, she said I hadn't, so I told her I wanted to be christened. Mum said, if that's what I wanted to do, I could be. I thought surely this would help me to be a good person and perhaps I would not be hanged one day like Dad had said.

'Mum,' I asked, 'why don't all of us children get christened?'

She replied, 'Don't be daft!' But she thought about it and eventually said, 'yes'. She then went to see the vicar at the Methodist church and the following week Mum held Joyce in her arms and we children, Norman, Kenny, David and me, all lined up for the service and to be sprinkled with the holy water. Dad did not attend.

Things settled down for a while but there was always an undercurrent of tension, especially if Dad had heard that George and the Old Girl had been to see Mum. He would question her as to whether they had set foot in the house; they had not. Mum always put a chair on the front step for Nan and she would make a cup of tea and a sandwich for them and give a shilling or two to George. People would walk past the house and have a good nose at them sitting there and then some nosey parker would tell Dad they had been to the house.

One sunny day Mum said we were all going to 'The Scrubs' for a day out. This was to see trainee parachutists jumping out from a small basket attached to a barrage balloon. Mum said this would be fun and Dad was to come, too. 'The Scrubs' was a wide area of waste ground near to Wormwood Scrubs prison. The large grey barrage balloon could be seen for miles around and we enjoyed watching the men float to the ground. Mum had brought a picnic of bread and jam, Smith's crisps and lemonade. When the boys got fed up with watching the men jumping, they were happily occupied with trying to catch the crickets and grasshoppers. But there was still tension between Dad and me so we still did not have much to say to each other.

Dad began to work on Sundays as a security watchman on the gate at the 'Crypto' factory. Mum said he would be hungry working all day and, as he did not like taking sandwiches, she wanted me to take his Sunday dinner to him.

'Do I have to?' I moaned.

'Yes you do,' she insisted. 'And I won't take no for an answer.'

This meant quite a long walk to the bus stop to wait for the bus; buses were not frequent on Sundays so I had to make sure I was there on time. I had given up on Sunday school as I was always arriving too late. I was reluctant at first to take Dad's dinner to him as he hardly ever spoke to me, but I did as I was told. Mum wrapped the dinner in a few tea towels and old newspapers then she put it all into a brown paper carrier bag and off I went, trying hard not to spill the gravy on the way. The streets around the industrial areas were so quiet on Sundays, with hardly a soul about, that it was as eerie as a ghost town – so different from the weekdays, when hundreds of people would be walking or riding their bikes to work. Dad and I did try to get on a little better and he was always pleased to have his dinner brought to him.

On the way home from the industrial area the bus stopped

outside a large Catholic church. I was curious as to what was beyond the big carved, wooden doors. On Sunday mornings there were always swarms of people, a lot of them Irish, leaving the church after the service and then most of the men folk headed to the nearest pub. There were so many men in the pub that they would spill out onto the pavements with their beer glasses in their hands and a lot of laughter and good humour going on. I wanted to know what had happened in the church to have made them behave this way when they came out. I decided to take a look inside the church. I pushed open the heavy doors and went inside this mysterious musky place. Apart from the dim daylight coming in through the stained-glass windows, there were dim spotlights highlighting the paintings of the saints. At the front was the blue-and-white covered altar with a large brass cross in the centre. There was also a statue of Mary in a long blue gown. On the other side of the church there was another statue of Jesus on a cross, further along was a picture of him with his chest open, exposing his heart. I didn't like the penetrating eyes in the pictures looking down at me; they were scary. Could they see into my soul and see what sort of person I was? I looked quickly away then strolled about the church, walking up and down through the wooden pews as if I was a wandering, invisible spirit or ghost. Each time I passed by the altar I bobbed up and down and crossed my chest as I thought this was what I was supposed to do. I noticed a small wooden cubicle, and took a look inside. There was a button. I pressed it and when I heard a rustling noise as if someone was coming, I ran out of that place as fast as I could. The place was creepy and I did not understand why so many people would go into there and why they seemed so happy when they came out.

Just before my fourteenth birthday, I went as usual to the 'Crypto' with Dad's dinner. Dad took the dinner from me and took it into the office, then he came out and said for me to come with him. We went round to the back of the office building and there propped up against the wall was a beautiful, maroon, drop-handle lady's bicycle. I was puzzled as to what such a lovely bicycle was doing there.

'Go on, take a good look,' said Dad kindly.

'It's lovely!' I said, running my finger over the saddle.

'It's yours!'

'What?' My jaw dropped; I did not understand.

'It's yours,' Dad repeated, 'but you can't take it home yet, not until you learn to ride it.'

I was shocked and could hardly take in what Dad was saying. I had always wanted a bike and this one was a beautiful Raleigh with gears, a saddlebag and dynamo lights.

'Yes, it's all yours. I have been saving up to buy it for you.'

I couldn't thank Dad enough, not just because he had bought me a bicycle but that he had been working overtime on Sundays to buy it for me. I knew then he must like me and not hate me, as I thought he did. I understood then that he had not had any training in how to be a father to a tearaway like me and just did the best he could, not only for me but for all of his family.

I got up onto the bike and Dad held the saddle as I wobbled along. I fell off a few times but eventually I had the hang of it. I rode around the whole factory, in and out past the machines, through the offices up and down through the centre of the factory, ringing the bell over and over with excitement. I rode around until I was confident. Dad showed me how to take the tyre off, how to mend a puncture and how to pump the tyres up. He showed me all the hand signals and how to manoeuvre when turning right. He spoke about road safety and traffic lights and for me to make sure I always put the padlock on when I wasn't using it. This was the first time Dad had ever spoken to me like this. I felt as if he was being like a proper father now and not treating me like a little kid. We then rode home together, Dad on his bike and me on mine, father and daughter. I was so happy that day.

Now I had a bicycle I made friends with a girl from our road named Judy King who also had a bike. Judy was a sensible girl and the envy of many girls in our road, as she had the loveliest golden ringlets hanging right down her back. Her mother tied up her hair every night in rags to make her hair form tight curls. I had grown my hair longer now and tried to make ringlets myself, but my hair was too thick and just fell down straight again. Mum was happier now there was a truce between Dad and me, and I was also calmer and not so rebellious now I had my bike. Mum bought me a pair of white shorts to match Judy's and she knitted a white bobble hat. Judy and I rode to many places together including Richmond, where we took our shoes off and paddled in the Thames.

Whatever the weather was like at the weekends, I rode around the centre of London to Trafalgar Square, Hyde Park, down The Mall to Buckingham Palace and on to Kensington, past Harrods and all the posh shops. I loved my bike; it was like being set free. I loved the feel of the wind on my face and through my hair. I also cycled every day to school which saved on my bus fare.

One day I was riding down the road towards home when I saw a familiar figure waiting on the doorstep. It was Billy.

Chapter 16

Billy stood awkwardly with his hands in his pockets.

'Hello, Rosie,' he said with a sheepish smile. 'Where have you been, anywhere nice?' His face was thinner than I remembered and his large nose cast a shadow over his wide crooked mouth. Billy nodded towards the road. 'I'm just waiting for your Mum to come home. She has popped over to the corner shop to buy some sugar.' Billy was wearing a short, badly fitting grey jacket, blue shirt and a darker shade of grey flannels. He was now aged twenty-three.

I didn't want to go into the house alone but looking up the road I could see Mum just leaving the shop.

'Hello, Billy,' I said in an indifferent tone as I walked past him with my bike. He followed behind me. I parked the bike against the wall in the passage. 'What are you doing here, Billy?' I tried not to look worried. 'Are you coming back to live here?'

'No,' he replied. 'I'm only here to see your mum and the Old Girl, then I am going back to Manchester.'

'Well, that's good. You must like it up in Manchester.'

'Yes it's OK, but I have missed having a "do" with you,' he laughed.

' "A do"! You haven't changed much have you? What makes you think I would want a "do" with you?'

I did not wait for a reply but ran up the stairs and into my bedroom and put a chair under the handle.

I listened out to see if Billy had followed me but there was no sound of him.

Mum came in with her shopping and I could hear her talking to Billy.

I sat on the edge of my bed looking out of the window towards the houses and gardens that backed onto ours. The wind had blown a net curtain out from the sash window of one house and a hand was trying to reel it back in, succeeded, and then shut the window up. An old stone lion sat on the dividing garden wall, the deep crack in the neck of the lion just about holding the head against the body. Nan had scolded me when she lived here and I was in the back garden riding on the lion's back. She chased me with a broom when I slid off and she saw the gaping crack, 'You would break cast iron, you would,' she cried. I tried to explain that I had not made the crack in the lion, but she was in no mood to listen 'You bleeder, clear off and go play in the front garden and leave my lion alone.' I fled from her before the broom landed on my back.

'Are you in, Rosie?' I heard Mum call up the stairs. I opened my door; it looked clear so I ventured to the top of the landing.

'Yes, Mum,' I called back. Billy stepped out in front of me as if from nowhere. 'Well what about it then, shall we give it a go?'

'You are disgusting,' I spat.

'Come on, you must have missed me and you must have missed having a "do" - surely?'

He blocked my way and made a grab for me, one arm around my waist and the other on my breast. His body pressed against me and I panicked. 'Get off of me!' I said, struggling to free myself. 'Mum!' I shouted, 'Billy won't let me go and he is touching me.'

Above left: My father, Norman Handleigh.

Above right: My mother, Helen, holding me.

Left: Uncle Billy holding me. Billy would have been about 11 years old.

Above: Mum and Dad with me and my brothers, Norman and Kenneth (the baby).

Below: My father with me and Norman (front, centre) at Butlin's watching a swimming race.

Above: Me with Norman.

Below: Oldfield Road Junior School: our leaving school picture before we left to go to senior school. I am in a striped dress, 4th from left, middle row. The teachers in the picture are the headmaster, Mr Tickner, and Mrs Saunders

At Butlin's. Dad with Norman, me with Mum. The chalet was a small shed.

Above: Me, Norman and baby David

Left: Norman, me, Ken and baby David. I must have been about seven or eight.

These pictures were taken by the young man, Bobby, who lived across the road from us. He had TB and he struggled with breathing to take these pictures.

Above: Kenneth and me with mum at the Serpentine in Hyde Park (I think).

Left: Me in the back garden. I was about 10 years old.

Above: From the left: twins Pauline and Brenda Shepherd, me and Sylvia Shepherd. We had gone out for a bike ride (this is the only picture I have of the Shepherd girls).

Left: I love this picture of Norman (left); note his boots and jumper. I am in the middle with David, and Ken is on the right.

A school picture of me at about twelve.

Above: Me at the front, with a friend on our bikes. My mother knitted us the woolly hats.

Left: Me at age 16, after I had had Martin

Above: Me at Margate. I had gone there with Bobby, who had TB, and his parents. We had gone by car, the first time I had ever been in a car.

Left: This was my first swimsuit, it was pink and white.

Above: This was me in the new grey suit my mum bought me to start my first job in a ladies clothes shop.

Left: This is Martin at about five months old.

Me in the suit mum had bought me to start work in.

Billy let me go as if he had just burnt his hands. We stood staring defiantly at one another. I think my new inner strength scared him.

Mum shouted back up the stairs. 'Stop playing silly buggers and come on down now, both of you; I've bought some jam and nice fresh bread, so you had better be quick before the boys come in and finish it off.'

I suddenly felt a sense of freedom and strength, realizing I was no longer the helpless child I once was. 'I'm warning you, Billy. Don't ever touch me again or I will tell Mum and Dad about what you have done to me since I was little. I mean it: I will tell on you.'

Billy showed me the palms of his hands, shrugged his shoulders and pulled a face. I fled down the stairs as he said, 'You are getting too big for me anyway.'

I knew then I wouldn't have to worry about Billy ever molesting me again. I was glad when he went back to Manchester and hoped I would never see him again.

Back at school in the autumn my friend from school, Sheila Thomas, sometimes joined me and the other kids in our road. One evening we were all sharing bags of chips as we sat on a garden wall a few doors up our road. There were quite a few of us, including the Cobb boys and the Shepherd girls. We chatted and teased each other. Someone in the house outside where we had gathered banged on their window and told us to 'clear off'. We just laughed and moved to another garden wall. In my bedroom, Sheila and I had painted a black pen line up the back of our legs to give the illusion that we were wearing stockings. We also applied Max Factor Panstik make-up which we plastered thickly on our faces and then smoothed in before finishing off with lipstick, though we made sure it was all rubbed off before we went home, otherwise we would be in trouble with our parents. One of the Cobb boys handed me a cigarette. I wanted to look grown up, as if I was used to smoking. I puffed repeatedly; trying to smother my coughing, then I felt dizzy and I then was violently sick in the curb. Everyone laughed at me. I felt stupid and I didn't want to smoke again.

My other friend, Maureen Roberts from Burns Road, and I had started to visit a place near the gasworks to meet up with what was known as 'The Taylor's Lane Gang' They were a really rough crowd of about ten or more teenagers. They dressed, acted and looked tough and said they would fight with bicycle chains, dustbin lids and knuckledusters if need be. Their reputation was well known and other gangs steered clear of them. But nothing really happened as they just acted tough to frighten people off. We only saw one fight and that was just a punch-up with one of their own members. Maureen and I hung about for a few weeks with them, then gave up as we thought they were just all talk and no action and we had become bored with them and their silly 'big boys' act. The only thing they did well was to swear at each other.

My life changed again when Sylvia Shepherd and I went to see Billy Graham, the American evangelist, at Wembley Stadium football ground. The whole place was bursting at the seams with people who had come to witness Billy Graham's teachings about the Bible. Many people fainted and were carted off by the St John's Ambulance attendants. The service and atmosphere was electrifying and I had never seen anything like it before. People were making strange sounds, throwing their arms about and crying and moaning. Billy Graham asked people to accept Jesus into their life and to come down to the front of the stage. Sylvia and I went down and he asked us if we accepted Jesus. We were caught up in the entire hullaballoo and said eagerly, 'Yes we do.' We wanted this man named Jesus in our life more than anything. The news camera was there and filmed us girls laughing and giggling, but we did not mind. Pity is there was not much follow-up after we had said 'yes' to Jesus, other than a short letter and pamphlet through the post from a woman. So it was not long before I forgot all about Jesus, though I am sure he did not forget about me.

One dark autumn evening, I was debating whether to stay in as it had been raining heavily all day or to go out. If I were to stay in, I would have to put up with my noisy brothers; Dad was already getting annoyed with them as he said that all he wanted was a bit of peace and to listen to the wireless when he got home from working in the factory all day. If I were to make a noise, he would give me a fixed stare, which would make me feel uncomfortable. And if that didn't work, he would end up shouting at me, then Mum would most probably start. So, rain or not, I decided to go out. The rain had stopped when I stepped out of the house; I would go and call on Sheila to see if she wanted to come out. I rushed down the doorstep, my head bent down against the bitter cold. I collided with someone who was passing the house.

'Whoops sorry!' he laughed, catching me around the waist before we both fell. 'I didn't see you coming out of your house like a tornado.'

'I'm sorry,' I replied, steadying myself. 'I was not looking where I was going.'

I could pick out, with the light from the lamp post, a young man in a black longline drape jacket, drainpipe trousers, and a white shirt beneath a beige waistcoat with brass buttons. He had black hair brushed back at the side and a 'Tony Curtis' at the front. I could not make out the colour of his eyes as he had his back to the light, but I could see that he was the best-looking person I had ever met. He spoke with an accent I did not recognize. I felt embarrassed at this new strange feeling I felt inside and went to hurry away.

'Hold on a minute,' he said, 'what's the hurry?'

I stopped in my tracks and for the life of me I could not think of a good reason why I was in such a hurry. I nervously mumbled something about meeting my friends. He laughed and said they must be very special if I was in such a hurry.

'No not special,' I said.

He soon put me at ease and I desperately wanted to hear his funny accent again. We stood talking for a while and I learnt that his name was Tony Hawke; he was seventeen years old and he came from Cornwall. He said he was in London working as a fireman on the steam trains at Willesden Junction. Tony also said he had seen me before when I had been outside Maureen Roberts's house, where he was now lodging.

'I really like you,' he added, 'and now we know each other, can we start courting?'

I had never heard anyone say 'courting' before and could hardly stop myself from laughing. He looked hurt.

'No really it's all right; it's just your Cornish accent,' I giggled.

'Well?' He waited for an answer, but I did not know what to say as I had never had a boyfriend before – what exactly did that mean?

'Well?' he repeated. 'What's it to be: do we start courting or not?'

'Yes!' I blurted out. 'Yes, all right then.'

'Right you are then. I will call on you tomorrow at seven o'clock.' He bent forward and gave me a quick kiss on the lips, then walked off down the road. Stunned, I went indoors having forgotten where I had been going to go in the first place. How had this encounter with this young man stirred up such a strange feeling in the pit of my stomach and made me feel strange? I ran my finger along my lip thinking about the fleeting kiss he had given me.

Chapter 17

'What's been the matter with you today?' asked Sheila, as we came out of the school gates. 'You have looked half asleep or in a trance all day, so what's up?'

'I'm all right.' I hesitated then blurted out breathlessly: 'I met a boy last night and he almost kissed me.'

Sheila looked surprised. 'What do you mean, he *almost* kissed you? He either kissed you or he didn't.'

'Well, it was just a peck, not a proper smacker.'

Sheila jumped up and down with excitement. 'I knew it. I told you last week, didn't I? Didn't I?'

It was true. The previous week she had told me that at our age we would want to kiss boys soon and they would want to kiss us.

'I've kissed boys before,' I said.

Sheila looked surprised. 'What? A real kiss, like they do in the films?'

'No, just pecks. I don't know how to kiss someone like they do in the films and besides I have never had the opportunity to slobber someone and I don't think I would like to either,' I said.

'It can't be that bad and we will have to do it soon – we should practise.' We were sitting on a garden wall at the time and she leaned forward and kissed me on the lips. Shocked, I slid off the wall and faced her.

'Well,' she said, sliding off the wall and facing me, 'Do you want to practise or not?'

'Yes, of course. I suppose so.'

Sheila kissed me again.

'Well,' I said, 'was that all right?'

'No. It was too wet,' she said, wiping her lips. 'Try again but this time close your eyes.' We locked lips.

The kiss was soft and gentle and Sheila looked as if she had liked it. 'Right, I think we have now got it,' she said. 'Remember, Rose: boys don't want to feel as if they are kissing a wet fish.' We both laughed and I teased her by saying how does she know so much about kissing, but she just laughed again and said, 'Never you mind how I know.'

'Well,' said Sheila, bringing me back to reality. 'What is this boy like?' I told her quickly what I knew about Tony before telling her I must hurry home to get ready. Sheila gave me a wave goodbye 'Remember what I've said: dry kisses!'

'Yes, mam,' I laughed, giving her a salute as I rode away on my bike. 'I'll see you on Monday and tell you all about it.'

Mum looked worried when I told her I had a boyfriend and he was going to call for me that evening. She wanted to know all about him. Where I had met him, what age was he, what work did he do, where did he live. I laughed and said we had only just met and he was working on the railway.

'He's seventeen, almost eighteen, and his name is Tony, but people know him as "Hawkeye" on account of his last name being Hawke.' I was worried about telling her all this as, well... supposing he didn't call for me? What if he changed his mind, what if he had learnt all about George and my Nan from Mrs Roberts and decided he did not want to 'court' me after all.

'But you are only fourteen, Rose,' said Mum. 'You are too young for a boyfriend.'

'Don't worry, Mum. I can look after myself and anyway he may not even come here.'

I needn't have worried, though, as on the dot of seven he knocked on the front door. Mum told me I was to take him upstairs into the front room where it was tidier. I wore the black skirt that I had worn to school and a yellow cotton blouse I had made in the needlework class at school. I also wore a wide black elastic belt with a brass buckle and my black velvet plimsoll shoes. Tony wore the same suit he had had on the previous evening and a clean white shirt. He looked even more handsome in the light. The front room was quite cold but we sat next to each other on the sofa. Mum put on the television for us to watch and she fussed about with the cushions on the armchairs, not really knowing what to say to Tony. On hearing the television, my brothers came rushing in and sat on the floor. I felt uncomfortable as my brothers sat studying Tony instead of the television. David wore his wire-rimmed glasses and he tried to focus out of the weak eye that was not covered with the sticky plaster. His nose had a 'green candlestick' hanging down which he tried to snort back up his nose. Kenny carried his collection of old shoes and lined them up to play 'cars'. Norman sat sucking on a slice of bread. At eight thirty Tony got up and said he had to go. We said good night on the doorstep and Tony kissed me lightly and said he would see me the following day. I just hoped my lips were not wet.

The neighbourhood gossip soon got round that Rose Handleigh had a boyfriend, but we didn't care about what people said as we were proud to be seen together and we linked arms as we walked along the road. Tony never once tried to go any further than a kiss, holding hands or putting his arms around me. At first when Tony hugged me I pushed him away, almost in a panic; he asked what the matter was and I replied there was nothing the matter and put my arms around his waist and we gently kissed. Gradually, over time, I learnt to trust him not to take advantage of me.

97

Maureen Roberts was really annoyed when she found out Tony and me were together. Tony said she was jealous as she thought she would have had a chance with him herself, as he was lodging with her family. Maureen was also upset because I did not see her as often as I was spending so much of my time with Tony. Tony and I were very happy with each other and spent a lot of time going for walks and talking about his family in Cornwall. When it was snowing we stayed indoors cuddling up on the settee but when we stayed in we were hardly ever alone. And if the boys were not hanging around, my dad would be spying through the crack in the door to make sure there was no hanky-panky going on. He also crept quietly around the house so you never knew where he was. We went to the cinema on Fridays when Tony was not on late shift and we actually went upstairs in the two and sixes and sat in the back row and Tony put his arm around my shoulder and occasionally gave me a tender kiss. As Tony was approaching his eighteenth birthday, we knew he would soon be called up for National Service.

The call-up papers came just before his birthday. I was upset knowing he would be going away into the army as I would really miss him, though I tried to hide it from him.

'Don't worry, Rose, when I come out of the army we can get married and have lots of kids,' he joked.

A week later Tony came to the house and joyfully swung me round in his arms. 'I'm not going in the army,' he said, 'I was turned down on health grounds.'

Concerned, I replied, 'But what is the matter with you? Are you ill?'

'No I'm not,' he laughed. 'They tested my hearing and decided that I was deaf in one ear, so they turned me down.'

'But I didn't know you were deaf in one ear.'

'I'm not deaf. I just pretended to be deaf.'

'But that's an awful thing to do.' I put my arms around his

waist and squeezed him tight. 'But I'm glad you did. I don't think I could bear to be apart from you.'

In the March Tony went back to Cornwall for a few weeks to see his family. It was just as well, as Mum went into hospital and I was worried about her as I did not know what was wrong. Dad just said I was not to visit Mum as she would be home in a few days and I was to stay off school to look after the boys and Joyce.

At home a few days later I went into the living room with Joyce in my arms. Dad handed me a letter. Puzzled, I put Joyce down onto the settee. Dad carried on reading his newspaper whilst I opened it.

Dear Rose,

I am glad you are managing to look after the kids all right and I hope they are being good. Make sure Joyce has some milk before she goes to bed and don't give Norman bread before he goes to bed as he may choke if he sleeps sucking his bread. I will be home in a few days with a new baby sister. Be good till then.

Love from Mum x

I was stunned. I had no idea Mum was pregnant again. Her tummy was always big and round so she had not looked any different to me.

I could feel the anger rising in me. 'How could you have done this again, getting Mum pregnant when you know we are struggling to make ends meet?'

Dad put his paper onto his lap. 'Yeah! I know, but you know what your mother's like.' He looked pitiful.

'Don't you blame Mum,' I shouted. 'She didn't do this on her own, you know. Aren't ten pregnancies enough for you? You should be ashamed of yourself.'

Dads face, balding head and ears went a bright red; his blue eyes were blazing behind his brown-rimmed glasses. He stood up and I waited defiantly for the blow, vowing that if he hit me I would fight back.

'Don't you talk to me like that!' he retorted. 'It has got nothing to do with you.' He was face to face with me, but I would not back down. Joyce started to cry.

'Oh yes it does have something to do with me when you are slowly killing my mother with all these kids.'

Dad took a step back as if I had slapped his face, but I did not let up. 'Don't you think she has enough to do? Don't you think she has struggled enough to feed us all? How much longer has Mum got to buy the leftover scraps from the shops and go to the jumble sales to clothe us? So don't you dare say it has nothing to do with me and act as if you are innocent and didn't make her pregnant!' I screwed up the letter and threw it at him and ran out of the room. Joyce was left crying.

I stayed out of Dad's way for the next few days until Mum came home from hospital. I could hardly bear to look at the new baby or Mum. Mum told me her name was Joan and asked whether I would like to hold her. She laid her in my arms before I could answer. Baby Joan was sleeping peacefully. She had a pretty little face, a white knitted bonnet covered her dark hair, and a white shawl was wrapped around her. I softened; it was not this poor little mite's fault. Dad did not make a fuss of the baby or even look at her. It was after this that Dad moved out of their shared bedroom, saying he needed his sleep without being disturbed by a crying baby or Mum coughing herself sick every night. Dad never again shared a bedroom with Mum. A few weeks after Mum and the baby had come home from hospital Mum realized there was something not quite right with Joan. The baby was taken into Stanmore Orthopaedic Hospital as she had been born with problems to do with her bones, including dislocated hips and one arm that was shorter than the other.

Joan was in the hospital for the first few years of her life as she suffered one operation after another. Mum visited the hospital almost every week and sometimes I would go with her to see Joan and I'd become very upset when I saw the plaster casts on her poor little body.

Now I had a boyfriend and was growing up, I wanted money to buy new clothes. Mum could not afford to give me more than my two shillings pocket money a week so I went into every shop in the High Street to ask if they would give me a Saturday job. I was almost giving up asking when I went into a small café run by two elderly sisters. They said they would give me seven shillings and sixpence for doing the washing up and, if I washed the floor when the café closed at three o'clock, they would give me an extra nine pence. I was as pleased as punch at landing this job. As well as the money, the sisters gave me a dinner. It was a busy little café so there was always a pile of washing up to do. My hands were in water almost all of the time and I hated cleaning the meat tins, and the saucepans were such a job to get clean. My hands felt rough and my knees were ingrained with dirt after washing the floor. At three o clock I rushed to the shops. I spent the money as soon as I received it. I bought new stockings and underwear the first week, and then every Saturday afternoon my money was hardly in my pocket for two minutes before I spent it on buying new blouses or skirts. If I had any money left, I would buy a little something for Joyce.

Early in the summer on a hot day, Tony and I took the train from Willesden Junction to Richmond. We wandered hand in hand by the River Thames. Tony said the river was filthy and dirty, not like in Cornwall where the sea water and rivers were so pure you could see the fish swimming as clear as daylight. I thought he must have been exaggerating, as it surely was not possible to have water as clear as he had described; I had only ever known water in the rivers and ponds to be murky. Tony told me I would get a dreadful disease if I paddled in the water. I playfully splashed him and he splashed me back and we both ended up laughing. We were drenched to the skin and my hair hung like a rat's tail. The day was getting hotter so our clothes dried on us as we walked up to Richmond Park to look for deer. We eventually found a herd of deer, but they ran away when they knew we were there. Laughing and exhausted, we sat down in the long grass to rest.

'One day I will take you to Cornwall to see for yourself how clear the water is,' Tony said as he sat and chewed on a blade of grass. 'I'll take you to see my family in Truro. They will love you as I do, especially my ma and pa.' Laying down and stroking his back, I stared up at the clear blue sky.

'Do you really think they will like me?'

Tony threw the blade of grass away and lay down on his back beside me and he, too, studied the clear blue sky. 'Of course they will. I love you, so why wouldn't they?'

'I hope they will, as I love you, Tony, and never want to leave you,' I said.

He took me in his arms and we kissed, at first gently then passionately and eagerly.

'You are so beautiful,' he said between kisses. 'I so want you.'

I was overcome with the heat and my love for Tony and we made love for the first time. It was afterwards, when we strolled back to the railway station, that I realized that Uncle Billy had never actually had full intercourse with me.

'You all right?' said Tony worried 'What are you thinking about? You are not sorry are you? I do love you.'

'Yes I'm fine' I said, reaching up to give him a peck on the cheek. I was fourteen, in love and the world was right with me. After that day we could not get enough of each other; the floodgates were open and there was no going back to as we were. The summer was a magical time. We thought it would never end, but alas, nothing lasts for ever.

At the back of my mind I did worry about what would happen if Dad ever found out about Tony and me, as being underage there was no knowing what he would do to both of us; he might, I thought, even have us sent to prison. I was worrying about all this as I was working in the café. I would be fifteen soon and wished it could have been my sixteenth birthday and then it would not matter anymore. My ears pricked up at the news on the radio and I stopped scrubbing the meat tins. The news reader said that Ruth Ellis had been hanged that morning for killing her lover. The newsreader also said there were big demonstrations outside the prison gates as public opinion was that hanging should be abolished. I felt a shiver go through me: hadn't Dad said that one day I would end up on the end of a rope? How relieved I was when it was announced a while later that Ruth Ellis would be the last woman in Britain to be hanged.

Chapter 18

Nan would often come to the house, sometimes on her own and sometimes with George, though, as I've said, they were both forbidden to enter the house. Tony used to make Nan laugh with some of the things he said to her. Tony could hardly believe that Nan and George had been thrown out and were not allowed back into the house; he thought it was terrible that an old lady had been treated like she had been treated. I told Nan that I loved Tony and one day we would get married. She said she liked the look of him but warned me I would have many a broken heart before I would settle down and get married. I laughed at her and said, 'No I won't - we love each other and nothing would ever tear us apart.' Little did I know!

At last I left school for good. I was so pleased and relieved that I would never have to go to that wretched place again. A lot of the girls were crying at leaving the school, but I just said 'good riddance' as I had hated school and the spiteful teachers and their rules and regulations. I was still fourteen years old and, as I would be fifteen years old before the new term started, which was beyond the school leaving age, I was allowed to leave. A lot of girls in my year, however, were not allowed to leave until the following Christmas or Easter, depending on when their birthday was.

I left the job in the café and started full-time work in a ladies' fashion shop, Marian's, which was in the High Street. Mum bought me a new grey suit and blouse to wear for work. I felt so grown up and proud as I looked the smartest I had ever looked. Bobby saw me from his window when I was coming home from work that first day and called from the window. He said he had never seen me look so smart and said he would take my photo, which he did. Bobby looked so frail and ill; I felt sorry for him trying to catch his breath, so to cheer him up I told him all about my first day at work and how much I loved Tony. He just smiled and said for me to be careful and not to carry all my eggs in one basket.

The shop had only been open for a short while and was owned by a really posh couple who lived above the shop with their two children, a baby and a toddler. The manager and his wife worked in the shop whilst a nanny, dressed in a uniform, looked after the children and took them out for walks in a big bouncy pram. It was strange to see a nanny in full uniform in our district; I had only seen nannies with prams in Kensington Gardens and Hyde Park. The nanny had lots of strange looks from people. Another lady also worked in the shop; she was married to a Polish man that would meet her every day at 5.30 p.m., as she said he was very a very jealous man. When I was not serving customers I would be ironing the clothes, ready to go onto hangers or to be used on the dummies in the shop window. The shop had a long wooden and glass counter with lots of drawers beneath it, containing underwear and stockings. There were also drawers along the back wall full of blouses, woollen jumpers and cardigans. On Saturdays the shop was always very busy, and the 15-denier stockings sold like hot cakes, especially the ones with the fancy black seams up the back or the ones with patterns at the side of the ankle. When a particular size of stocking had sold out, I was asked to take other sizes into the back room and to rub off, with my finger nails, the logo and size at the top so they could still be sold to gullible people who would not notice that they did not have a size marked on them. I thought this was dishonest, but I was young and did as I was told. Thursday afternoon and Sunday was my time off as the shop would be closed. I earned £2.10s a week and I was happy to be able to give Mum a pound a week for my keep.

Tony and I were inseparable and spent as much spare time together as possible. He said to me that Maureen Roberts and her new friend, Josie, were forever trying to flirt with him. Tony said he could not stand the sight of either of them and wished they would leave him alone. I knew Josie's reputation as being a 'hard nut' and hoped I did not bump into her unexpectedly as we might have ended up having a fight.

Tony's friend Alan, who also worked on the railway, would sometimes come out with us to the park or pictures, and, although I did not mind at first, I soon got fed up with him hanging around when all I wanted to do was be alone with Tony. And, besides, I did not trust him.

I was proved right just after my fifteenth birthday. Tony and I were sitting in the front room and Mum and Dad came bursting in.

'Is it true what Mrs Roberts has just told us about what you two have been up to together?' Mum shouted angrily.

A shiver went down my spine. 'What are we supposed to be up to?'

Dad stormed over to me. 'Don't you act the innocent to me, my girl.'

Mum held Dad back when he turned to Tony and raised his arm. 'Don't, Norman!' she pleaded. Dad stopped and lowered his arm and said through gritted teeth. 'I suggest you get your backside out of here before I knock your block off.'

Tony opened his mouth say something. 'Go, Tony, go. I'll sort this out,' I cried.

'No you won't, my girl. I'll sort this out and I will be the one to sort him out after I've sorted you out,' said Dad.

I cried out to Tony as he fled that I would see him later.

'No you will not,' screamed Mum. 'You will never see him again, ever. Do you hear me?'

I began to cry.

'You will never ever see him again,' she repeated. 'If you do, we will go straight to the police station to report what you and he have been up to. You're underage and that means prison for him and a home for you.'

I started to sob loudly. They made me feel as if what we had done had been dirty and not an act of love. There was not a thing I could say or do; it would be pointless as they were so angry and I was so afraid of again being shut in a police cell.

I fled the room and ran to my bedroom and put the chair under the handle. I flipped onto the bed and cried and cried and tried to block out the ranting from Mum and Dad along the hallway. How did Mrs Roberts find out about this? The only one Tony had told was his friend, Alan, so he must have told Maureen and in turn she told her mother, who could not wait to tittle-tattle to Mum and Dad. I expect Maureen and her new friend Josie were pleased with themselves now. I could hear Mum and Dad still shouting that I had brought shame on our family and it would be all over the neighbourhood by now about what we had been up to. I didn't know what Mum and Dad had in mind to do about Tony and me. The suspense was a nightmare as I expected the police to come for me at any moment. But they wouldn't inform the police, said Mum later when she had calmed down, just as long as I promised not to see Tony again.

Mum came to meet me from work each evening, just in case I was to sneak off to meet up with Tony. When I got home I was to go straight to my room, which I was only too glad to do. Dad had searched my room whilst I was at work and he destroyed all the photos of Tony and he had taken all the love letters and thrown them away. The ache inside was so painful, and however many tears I shed it did not ease the pain. How could I live without Tony? My heart and soul felt empty, stripped, and nothing in my life seemed to matter anymore.

Mum did not stop nagging me at every opportunity she had. She told me Alan had told Mrs Roberts about what Tony and I had been up to, and now all the neighbours knew and I should be ashamed of myself for bringing this disgrace on the family and I was lucky the police had not found out.

A few weeks later, when Dad went to the club and Mum took the kids to the pictures, I heard someone at the front door and when I opened it was surprised to see Tony. We fell into each other's arms and then, hand in hand, we ran up the road. We ducked into the first alleyway we came to and smothered each other with kisses and overcome with passion we threw caution to the wind and made love against the wall.

Afterwards Tony walked home with me and then followed me indoors. I sat nervously on the bottom of the stairs. He sat next to me.

'Look, Rose, darling, come away with me. We can go to Cornwall and my ma will take care of us.' He put his arms around me. 'Please say yes and we can leave right now. I have enough money for our train fare... I love you so much.'

'I can't,' I said tearfully. 'They would only find us and we would be in a lot of trouble and maybe even go to prison' The thought of this filled me with horror. 'Tony, if you love me, go back to Cornwall to live with your ma and pa and when I am sixteen next August, come back for me.'

Tony pleaded with me but I was adamant and said 'no' and told him to go before my parents came back.

When he had gone I sat numb on my bed. I believed he would come back to me some day. I would wait for him. Why oh why could I not be sixteen now? I thought. Then we could be together without all this fuss. I hated my mum and dad for breaking us up. Didn't they realize that I might only be fifteen but I was old enough to know I loved Tony?

Weeks went by and I had not seen Tony around so I assumed he had gone back to Cornwall as I had asked him to do. One evening I was standing on the doorstep when Sylvia came out of her house. I had not seen her for some time. She said would I like to go to the park as the funfair was on. I asked Mum if it would be all right and she said it would be, so off we went. It was a very warm September evening and it was getting dark. Sylvia and I were walking aimlessly around the funfair, when, suddenly, through the crowd I saw a familiar figure walking, laughing, and with his arm around Maureen's friend, Josie. It was Tony. When they drew closer they stopped for a second. Tony went to say something to me but Josie pulled him along. Following them was Maureen cuddling up to Tony's friend Alan. Maureen gave a satisfied smirk as they passed by and then they were gone, swallowed by the crowd of happy people out enjoying themselves.

Shocked, I stood frozen to the spot, unable to say or do a thing. Sylvia tugged at my arm. 'Come on, Rose. It's time to go home.'

Chapter 19

The following weeks went by with me being in a very dark, emotional place. The pain wouldn't go. It twisted and gnawed at the pit of my stomach; it was like a dreadful illness inside of me. I had never imagined a broken heart could feel like this. Why had Tony, who said he loved me, started to see someone so soon, and with a person he had said he could not stand at any price? How could he have forgotten me already after we had been together for almost a year? Hadn't he agreed to come back to me on my sixteenth birthday? My days were an empty space now Tony had gone; I did not care about the world around me. I just knew I would never trust anyone ever again. I did not see or hear of Tony after that day at the funfair. And I can only assume he went back to Cornwall.

Billy came back to London for a few days only this time with a girlfriend, Shirley. Shirley was a plump girl of about twenty years old, she said 'Hello' in her Manchester accent, and she was pleasant enough. They said they were getting married in the springtime, possibly at Easter, in a registry office in Manchester, and we were invited. Shirley requested that we were to now call Billy by his proper name, the name on his birth certificate – John. I wondered if Shirley would still have married him if she knew what he had done to me. I went with them to Petticoat Lane on the Sunday as Billy wanted to show Shirley a proper old-fashioned London market. I did not want to go but Mum said she was going to see baby Joan in the hospital and asked me to show them the way. And, besides, she said, it would do me good to get out – I had been coming home from work and just shutting myself in the bedroom. Mum could see how unhappy I was and said time was a great healer and, given time, I would soon start to feel better.

It was a lovely sunny day and Billy, Shirley and I wandered from stall to stall. We absorbed the sounds, smells and atmosphere of the market. There were the cockney shouts from traders selling their wares and we breathed in the smell of the delicious foods, anything from buns to hot chestnuts. A photographer shoved a small monkey into Shirley's arms and took our photo. We laughed at the man standing on the back of a lorry selling china dinner sets. He threw the complete set, all at once, up into the air and then caught it without breaking a single thing. It was a fine art and the crowd was amazed and soon buying from him. 'Not for thirty pounds, not for twenty pounds, not even for fifteen pounds. No, hold on to your money, who will give me ten pounds for the lot?' Hands shot up waving their money, eager to buy before they were all sold out. Shirley and I bought five pairs of stockings each, which one of the traders was quickly showing us gullible people from his suitcase. I also bought a pair of pale-pink shoes. Billy and I waited outside while Shirley popped into the public toilet.

Billy turned towards me and put his hand on my shoulder. 'Rose, you won't tell Shirley about us, will you?'

'Why shouldn't I tell her, Billy? What you did to me for all those years was wrong. You know that, don't you?'

He shrugged his shoulders and gave me a pathetic sad face. I actually felt sorry for him.

'No, Billy,' I said. 'Your secret is safe. I won't say anything, but only on the condition that I never have to call you John.'

111

He looked relieved and nodded.

When we arrived back home and excitedly looked at our purchases, the stockings had ladders in them and the bottom of the shoes was made of cardboard instead of leather. But we had enjoyed the hustle and bustle of the market and I had forgotten my heartache. I was also relieved when they went back to Manchester, as I still did not trust Billy not to lunge at me if he had the chance.

I left the fashion shop when a girl I knew vaguely and who worked in a radio and television shop at the other end of the High Street told me that they wanted a new shop assistant as she was leaving to work elsewhere. When I arrived for the interview I hesitated before going in to study the board in the shop doorway showing a list of all the top-selling records. The shop manager introduced himself as John Kent. I liked him straight away; he was very polite and courteous. He beckoned me to sit at his desk at the far end of the shop. I guessed he was aged about twenty-four or -five. He had black hair and dark-brown eyes; he wore a dark suit, white shirt and blue tie. Mr Kent explained to me that hire purchase was now very popular and the job meant a lot of figure work. I said I was sorry but I was not much good at doing sums and I got up to leave. Jobs were easy to come by then and I was not too worried whether I got the job or not.

He smiled and asked me to sit down again. 'Don't go yet. I can offer you the job of selling records if you would like.'

I agreed and started work the following Monday. The shop was so much busier than the ladies' clothes shop and I enjoyed the variety of people that came in. Older people were now taking advantage of the hire purchase scheme and buying the televisions and radios. Younger people were coming in to buy record players and records. I soon learnt all the top-ten selling records by heart. John Kent was always very busy running the shop, serving and working out customers' hire purchase payments so he did not have much

112

time to spend with me after showing me how to do the job. John Kent's brother, Joseph, also worked in the shop and they would speak to each other in Armenian as they were Armenian Cypriots. Once or twice I noticed John Kent looking over at me as if he was deep in thought but I did not pay too much attention as I assumed he must have been mentally working out his accounts.

A few weeks after I started work in the shop, commercial television started. There was lots of excitement in the press, but as a lot of people did not have a television and the general opinion was that it would never catch on if the programmes had to keep stopping for advertisements to be shown, so no one was that excited about it. A furniture store in the High Street had a poster in the front window inviting people to come into the store to watch ATV for the opening performance. Mum, my brothers and I went along. I sat with the kids on a rolled-up carpet or, to be more precise, we sat on the carpet after the kids had finished jumping up and down on the new beds and walking up and down on the rolled-up carpet. Mum sat on a new armchair munching a sandwich and then Sharps toffees, which she handed around to us, much to the salesman's horror. We watched the opening ceremony, on a 12-inch television, launched from the Guildhall, followed by a variety show and excerpts from plays and ending with the National Anthem. We all laughed when the first commercial came on – it was for Gibbs toothpaste. One of my favourites was the Camay advert: a lady in a bath full of bubbles and a gentle, persuading voice singing, 'You'll look a little lovelier each day with wonderful pink Camay.' It was not long after this that people realized that commercial television had much more appealing programmes to offer such as variety shows and game shows than what the stuffy BBC had, and television sales began to thrive.

It was very busy in the shop and the records were selling so well, especially Bill Halley's 'Rock around the Clock'. A young man of about eighteen years old came into the shop quite often and always tried to spend more time than he should asking about various music and one day he asked if he could take me to the pictures. I thought, why not?, and said he could meet me from the shop the following day. I told Mum I would be going to the pictures straight from work so not to worry if I was late.

She said, 'I hope you are not arranging to meet Tony.'

'Don't be daft! I got over him ages ago and besides I heard he has gone back to Cornwall.'

After work the young man, Michael, was waiting for me. He wore blue jeans which were now all the fashion and a long drape jacket over a white shirt. He said he was going into the army in a few weeks' time. We went to the Odeon, and afterwards, on the way home, I told him I lived in St John's Avenue and he asked me if I lived near that crazy family: 'You know the one, where the old woman and her nutty son got thrown out.' I was embarrassed and lied, 'No, I live further down the road so I didn't know them.' Mick, as he preferred to be called, walked me to the bottom of the road. I stopped and said to him that he had better not take me to the door as my father was very strict and did not like me going out with boys. He kissed me goodnight and asked to see me on the Saturday. I agreed to meet him by the paper shop at the bottom of our road. I was feeling very uneasy lying to him about where I lived. I did not really want to go out with him now as he might find out where I lived and he might also have heard the rumours about me and Tony. I decided I would have to let him down gently as he was going into the army. On the Saturday Mick's face lit up when he saw me coming down the road towards him and before I could say anything he held my arms and gave me a kiss first on the cheek then gently on the lips.

'I'm so pleased to see you; I thought you might not come as your father is so strict.'

'No, it's fine. He thinks I am out with a friend,' I lied.

'Anyway,' he said, 'I have arranged for us to go to my house to meet my parents.'

I did not know what to say. This was moving too fast for my liking.

When we arrived at the house his mother was over-excited, as if I was the first girlfriend he had ever taken to meet them. I was shown into the living room where his father was already sitting at a table that was laden with very nice flowered plates and cups and saucers on a white linen tablecloth. Mick's father said 'Hello' and beckoned me to sit down. His mother went into the kitchen and came out with a plate of sandwiches followed by a plate of homemade jam tarts and iced fairy cakes. I felt very embarrassed again when Mick told his mother and father I lived in the same road as the 'crazy family'. His father laughed, 'Oh I remember "Dog End Dick". He would sometimes pass by here searching for the fag ends. What a state he was, wearing all those trousers tied up in the middle with string.'

Embarrassed, I could not eat a thing and just slowly sipped at the tea.

'Come on, eat up,' said his father, offering the plate of jam tarts to me. 'Michael's mother has spent all afternoon baking these.'

'Sorry, I am not that hungry,' I mumbled. 'I had dinner before I came out tonight.'

'Oh well, it's your loss,' he said taking another one himself.

I could sense that I was not making a good impression and was relieved when it was time to go. Mick walked me to the bottom of the road. We stopped and Mick was quiet for a minute as if he wanted to say something to me.

'What's the matter?' I asked. I wanted to tell him that I did not want to see him again but could not find the words.

'It's just that I want to ask you to be my girlfriend and for you to wait for me until I have finished National Service. We could write to each other while I'm away.'

I put my head down, wondering how to get out of this. Perhaps I could wait until he had gone then write a 'Dear John' letter to him.

'What's it to be then? Please say yes.'

I nodded 'yes' before he kissed me.

'One more thing,' he said. 'Are you a virgin?'

Shocked, I said, 'What! Why do you ask me that?'

'Well, are you?'

'Of course I am!' I lied. We said goodnight and agreed to meet up the following Friday.

'Did you have a good evening,' said Mum when I went indoors.

I rushed up the stairs, calling back, 'Yes thank you.' I closed my bedroom door and fell onto the bed crying. Was it always going to be like this, every boy I meet wanting to know every detail about me and wanting to have only a lily-white virgin as their girlfriend?

It was very busy in the shop on the Friday with teenagers coming in to buy the latest 78 rpm records after collecting their wages. I was dreading home time as Mick would be outside the shop waiting for me and I knew I would have to tell him that I did not want to see him again. Mr Kent closed the shop; I was lingering in the back room where I had gone to collect my coat when he came in.

'Are you not going home?' he said, picking up his keys from the table.

'Yes in a moment,' I said sadly.

'What's the matter, Rose? Why are you not rushing out as usual?' I was almost in tears and he pretended he had not noticed. 'Well, you had better hurry as your young man is waiting outside for you.'

'That's the problem,' I said, putting my coat on. 'I don't want him to be my "young man" and I don't know how to tell him as he is going into the army soon.'

'Oh dear, I can see why that's a problem then.' He thought

for a moment. 'Look, you stay here and I will go and have a word with him.'

'What could you say to him? It's me that has the problem, not you, and I will have to deal with it.'

John Kent rushed out before I could say any more. A while later he returned. 'All done – he's gone.'

'But what did you say?' I looked even more worried.

'I told him that you were sorry and that you were now going out with me.'

'Oh!' I said, shocked. 'What did you say that for?'

'That was the only way to get rid of him. That is what you wanted, wasn't it?'

'Well yes.'

'Come on, I will give you a lift home.' He picked up his keys again and, after locking up, he took me home in his small blue van. When we stopped outside of the house he asked me not to rush out. 'Would you like to come out to dinner with me?'

'Oh!' I said, surprised. 'Yes all right – when?'

'Now if you like.'

'Oh!' I said again. 'All right but I will have to tell my mum first.'

'Call me John,' he said after I got back into the van after telling Mum I wouldn't be late home.

John drove to Swiss Cottage where he said there was a really good Chinese restaurant. I had never even seen a foreign restaurant before, let alone gone into one. It was small and very posh inside with tables covered with white tablecloths with another blue one over the top and laid with silver cutlery and wine glasses. John ordered as I didn't have a clue what to order. The dinner looked like a bowl of dishwater with a bird's nest in the middle. It tasted revolting. There was also a side plate with boiled rice on it. The only rice I had ever had was in a rice pudding. But I was thankful that Aunty Ann had taught me how to handle cutlery: 'The soup spoon you tip away from you and you start from the outside knife and fork and work your way in. And don't forget that you don't hold the knife and fork like you would a pencil!' she would say.

John asked me what I would like to drink and I whispered to him that I was still only fifteen.

'Sorry, I keep forgetting how old you are, as you look and act so much older.'

I knew this to be true as lots of people mistook me for being older.

'But I would like a Babycham.' I had seen the adverts for Babycham and I thought it was a really sophisticated drink to ask for.

After dinner John drove me home. I said, 'Thank you and good night. I will see you tomorrow in the shop.'

John put his arm around me and much to my surprise he gave me a gentle kiss on the lips.

'Goodnight,' he said. 'See you in the morning.'

Chapter 20

The following day was really busy in the shop and John and I only had time to smile occasionally at each other in passing. At the end of the day I said goodnight as usual and left. This was how it was for the following week.

A romance with John was the last thing on my mind. He was too old for me, I reasoned; he must be at least twenty-five and from a different world to mine. John was a nice, kind, clever and intelligent person compared to me. I felt comfortable when he was in the shop and thought he had only taken me out to dinner that once because he felt sorry for me after telling Mick it was over. Saturday, as the shop was closing, John asked me if I would like to go out that evening with him. I was surprised but agreed. We went to a party at the house of one of his friends. There was a mixture of people, mostly Armenians. I could not understand what they were talking about as they did not speak in English. John sat beside me and held my hand and told me about the struggles of his country, how the Turks at the beginning of the century had killed so many Armenians, and how his family had moved to Cyprus to escape. John said he had another brother besides Joseph, who was still in Armenia fighting for the rights of Armenia. He said his family was now worried about the unrest in Cyprus as they still had family and friends there. I was mesmerized by what he was telling me and amazed that someone like John could treat me as an adult. I had never been worried about the state of the world as it seemed far away from my existence.

The following week John took me home to meet his mother and father. The terraced house was in a busy main road near to Neasden railway station. John let us in and took me along the passageway into the kitchen. John's mother was a small lady and neatly dressed in a green dress and wearing an apron which she untied and threw onto the back of the kitchen chair before giving John a hug. John's father was only a little taller than his wife. They both smiled and said 'Hello' to me in English. I held out my hand and said, 'Pleased to meet you Mr and Mrs Kent.' John laughed and explained the family name was Cholakian and only he had changed his name when he came to England; and that, in any case, his mum and dad did not speak English. John's mother showed us into the tastefully furnished living room and said she would make us a drink. I asked for coffee. She brought the coffee in to us on a wooden tray. The cups were like a doll's tea set and the coffee was thick and tasted vile. John said it was Turkish coffee. John kissed me gently on the lips when he took me home.

We began to see each other after work. I introduced him to my mum and she thought he was really handsome and I was surprised I did not receive a lecture from her. Dad did not say anything to me; he just buried his head in the newspaper whenever I was around. I told John about my nan and how she had been evicted and John said he would like to meet her as she sounded a character. We met Nan in the centre of London and went for something to eat in the A.B.C. teashop near Baker Street and then we went to see a show at the London Palladium. There was a comedian on and Nan did not like him or the female singer either, but she did like John. Nan thought he had the looks of a film star and said his brown eyes were so expressive.

One day, just after Christmas and just before closing time in the shop, John handed me a small brown box. I thought it was a late Christmas present and was puzzled as he had already bought me a yellow cardigan. The box contained a three-diamond crossover gold ring. I was puzzled and quickly handed it back to him.

He pushed it back to me. 'No, have a good look,' he said excitedly. 'What do you think of it?'

'But what is it for?' I said stupidly.

'It's an engagement ring, silly. Look, the shop is closing in five minutes; just hold onto it until later.'

I didn't know what to think. Did it mean he had a girlfriend he wanted to get engaged to and he wanted my opinion of the ring? Or did it mean he wanted to become engaged to me? No it couldn't be! My mind was in a whirl. John knows how old I am and we come from such different backgrounds and I am far too young for him anyway, so what is this all about?

After we left the shop John drove me, in his small blue van, to a Greek restaurant in Swiss Cottage, not far from the Chinese one we had gone to before. We did not say a word to each other on the way there. When we were seated I handed back the ring and asked him who it was for. He laughed and said, 'For you of course!'

'Oh!' was all I could say.

'Is that it? I am asking you to become my fiancée.' He could see I was concerned but continued: 'I know you are only fifteen but you seem so much older and mature for your age.' John took my hand and his words were coming out in a rush. 'You are so lovely and funny and beautiful. I would like for us to get married in the Armenian Church in Kensington when you are of age. That's if you agree. I do love you and am afraid you will go off with someone else if I don't make my feelings for you heard now.'

'Oh!' I said again. 'But what would my parents say?'

The waiter stood by to take our order. Greek music was being played by a couple of musicians in the corner of the small restaurant. John ordered for both of us, as yet again I did not have a clue what the dishes were.

'I will ask your parents first thing tomorrow. That is, if you will have me.'

'Well yes, all right I will.' So there I was at fifteen, engaged to be married. I did not feel the same way as I had done for Tony, but John was a lovely person and I felt safe and comfortable with him. He was also clever and intelligent, and Mum and Nan liked him and he was also very good-looking.

'But why now, John?' I asked. 'Shouldn't we wait until I am of age?'

'No, because I have seen the way other men look at you and I don't want you to see anyone else. I am changing my job soon as I want to start my own business and open up my own shop, that's why I am asking you now.'

The food arrived. It was rice wrapped up in leaves and there were various pieces of meat.

'They are vine leaves, Rose, and pieces of lamb,' John said as I gingerly took a bite into the little packages.

Some people do eat strange things, I thought. Supposing John would want me to cook these strange things when we do get married.

When we finished eating, a man with his female companion, who were seated at the next table, threw a plate on the floor and it smashed into little pieces just in front of three Greek men in traditional costume who had just begun to dance. I was startled, thinking there was going to be trouble, but the dancers took a plate from the pile on a table and smashed it onto the floor as well and danced around it. Then other people took a plate and smashed it. John picked up his plate and threw it.

'What's happening?' I said, laughing and joining in by throwing my plate. Everyone was laughing as all hell broke loose and plates flew all over the floor. 'It's the Greek tradition to smash plates after eating!' John shouted above the noise.

Then, linking arms, we all joined in the Greek dancing that became faster and faster until we all fell about laughing and exhausted onto the floor.

A few weeks later John and his brother Joseph gave up working in the shop to start work elsewhere. Changing employment was not unusual in our part of London as there was always plenty of work about. I missed John and Joseph when they left and I didn't want to be in the shop with new people, so when I heard about another job in a factory with bigger wages, I took it. The factory was about three miles away, and not on a bus route so I had to walk on the dark winter mornings through an alleyway running through Willesden Junction. The factory was a large warehouse full of looms making horsehair sacking that was used for divan beds. The noise was so deafening we had to wear earmuffs. Up and down the looms went all day long, sending an eight-inch metal bullet backwards and forwards to weave the material. My job was to thread the horsehair string into the bullet if it came flying off the machine, which it often did. It was a wonder how someone didn't get killed when this large metal bullet came flying through the air. I stuck this job out for a couple of weeks until one day the machine caught fire and everyone started running about like headless chickens to get the fire buckets to put the flames out. I ran to the door to escape the flames but the supervisor shouted and pointed for me to get another bucket. I thought, 'Sod you, I'm not going to end up cooked in this hellhole,' so out I went and did not go back.

My next job was in a factory in Acton, named Chesebrough Ponds. The factory was an enormous, amazing place and a hive of activity. I noticed there was a smell of oil and grease mixed with the smell of pork sausages and meat pies that drifted in from the Walls factory next door. The end products at Chesebrough Ponds were jars and tins of Vaseline, hair cream, hair tonic and shampoo. Each production line almost stretched the width of the factory floor. The noise from all of the machines was like an orchestra of different sounds, click-click, swoosh-swoosh, bang, rattle, clash, bump, grind and the clinking of glass upon glass and the odd sound of a jar or bottle smashing on the concrete floor. Each machine action was connected to the next; part of this chain was the people who worked there. The workforce was mainly young single women, as women were cheap labour as they always earned less than a man would. The few married women who were working there were considered to be earning 'pin money' for little extra treats, as it was still considered that a married man's duty was to be able to support his family whilst the woman stayed at home to run the house and look after the children. Everyone in the factory wore white overalls, hair tied back and a white starched head band on top fastened by hair grips. A few men, in brown overalls, worked the forklifts and there were also the maintenance men ready to assist if a machine broke down. My first duty was unpacking glass jars and putting them onto a metal wheel that then shuffled them around and pushed them onto a moving conveyer belt in neat rows of forty across. They were then filled with liquid Vaseline, from a machine which dropped down a line of small taps. The journey continued on the slowly moving conveyer belt until the Vaseline was set. A woman, sitting on a high stool, inspected the hundreds of bottles as they passed for any jars that had not been completely filled, or had dirt or oil on the top; in which case, they would be removed and discarded. The next stage for the jars would be the machine which put on the lids then the labels, before the bottles rolled onto another conveyer belt to be retrieved by more women to pack into boxes, which were then put onto pallets for the forklift truck to take away to be stored elsewhere.

Some days a maintenance man, named Sid, used to drink a jar of the liquid Vaseline, as he said it was good for him. Just the thought of this made me feel sick. The other production lines of hair tonic, shampoo and hair cream were run on the same principle; only the labels were put on by someone very quickly, putting the bottles into a slot for the machine to wet and stick the labels. The women at the end of the production line had to be very quick, otherwise the bottles and jars would pile up and slow the machines down. Sometimes it was as if you had become a part of the machines – everyone had a part to play and was just a link in the process. Each morning and afternoon we were treated to fifteen minutes of the radio variety show *Workers' Playtime*, when popular band music was played through the loudspeaker system and the women would sing along. There was also the opportunity to put your name down on a list to have your hair done, free of charge, in the treatment room. A woman would part your hair down the middle and wash one side with one shampoo and the other side with another, then test your hair and scalp to see if there was a reaction of any sort.

John had told my mum that we were engaged and she had told John it was best not to tell my dad as he would be furious. We agreed to keep it quiet as we did not want to create a scene with him, so I only wore my engagement ring when John and I were together. As I now did not work on Saturdays, I was able to enjoy spending the extra money I was earning, which was four pounds a week, at Shepherd's Bush market or in Oxford Street. Saturday evenings I dolled myself up to go out with John. I wore a new skirt or blouse, rubbed Max Factor Panstik into my face, then applied eye shadow and finished off by spitting on a small black block of mascara and rubbing a small brush across it to paint onto my eye-lashes. Sundays we spent either going to John's relatives or at his or my home.

Chapter 21

John and I saw each other almost every evening. We enjoyed each other's company and we spoke about the future and the work we were now doing.

John was a qualified electrical and television and radio repair person. He wanted to open his own shop with living accommodation above for us to move into after we were married. We went to look at a few shops but they were unsuitable as they were not in the main shopping areas or not big enough. John's brother Joseph wanted to share a business with John, but he would not discuss anything with me around as he did not approve of our relationship; he thought I was too young for John. Their younger sister, Salina, who was about nineteen years old, was always pleasant towards me.

At the beginning of March Mum told me poor Bobby from across the road had died of the TB. This really upset me. Bobby was so young and he had suffered so much. John held me in his arms when I cried, and said Bobby was now out of his pain. Mum also said we were going to Manchester in a few weeks, at Eastertime, as Billy and Shirley were to be married on 30 March. It was going to be a small registry office wedding and afterwards we were to go to Shirley's mother's house for tea. We would be staying with Aunty Ann who had now made a new life for herself in Manchester and seemed to have forgotten all about the previous family that she had left behind in London. She now lived with Tony, the Welshman, as a married couple and Ann had taken his surname, Davies. They now had two children, a boy, Paul, who was about three years old, the same age as Joyce, and a girl of about two who was also named Joan but was nicknamed Bobby. I protested to Mum that I did not want to go to Manchester but Mum would have none of it; she said Dad could not go as he was working and I had to help with the kids. I reluctantly agreed to go as I knew Mum would not be able to handle the children on her own. Mum said that if I were to see the Old Girl I was not to tell her about the wedding as she was not invited in case she caused trouble.

We travelled by bus to Victoria coach station for the overnight coach journey. Once on board the coach the boys were excited and noisy, much to the annoyance of the other passengers. I nursed Joyce and eventually the rocking movement and drone of the engine sent them all to sleep, including Mum. I could not sleep as I found it very uncomfortable and my neck ached and the journey made me feel sick. I studied my reflection in the window and noticed my face looked thin and drawn. My eyes, although I had eye make-up on, looked dark and heavy. I guessed this must be because of the long days at the factory and the late nights with John; I just wasn't getting enough sleep. Mum had been bellowing at me in the mornings to hurry up and get myself out of bed and washed and dressed before I was late for work. Lately on Saturday mornings I had been staying in bed until midday. The coach windows were now steaming up so I rubbed a patch and pressed my nose to the window but it was pitch black; the small sleepy villages came and went. I eventually dozed off. Dawn broke as we pulled into Manchester coach station and Mum and I struggled off of the coach and into the bitter cold and early mist with the four sleepy children, a pushchair for Joyce and three bags and my small suitcase. Mum pulled her knitted hat down over her ears and wrapped her long knitted scarf around her neck. Her coat almost reached her ankles, she never wore stockings and her lace-up shoes were flimsy. The boys were dressed in very thin trousers and jackets and they stood half asleep and shivering. I put Joyce down onto the pavement and then put the bags onto the pushchair. Joyce cuddled up to my legs as we waited for the early-morning bus to take us to Moss Side, where Ann and Tony lived. Ann was waiting at the front door of one of the long line of terraced houses. She had her apron on over her dress and a satin scarf tied in a turban around her head to hide the silver metal curlers and she had on calf-length suede boots.

'Tea's made' said Ann, giving Mum a hug. Then turning to us, she added, 'Come in all of you and warm yourselves up by the fire, and if anyone wants the toilet first, it's upstairs.'

Ann showed us in through the small lobby and into the lounge. The highly polished sideboard with a few ornaments was against one wall, and a matching heavy-looking table, with ball feet and chairs, was against another. There was a glass vase in the centre of the table but it held no flowers as I suppose flowers were too dear that time of the year. A wooden tray was also on the table with a brown teapot covered with a green knitted tea cosy, and cups and saucers. A small beige-coloured settee, which matched the two arm-chairs, was near to the open fireplace that looked as if it had only just been lit. We all warmed up nicely and munched on the toast Ann had cooked under the grill in the small kitchen.

Afterwards Norman, Ken and David made their way out into the backyard and they climbed up onto the wall to study the back alleyway. It was not long before the noise from the boys had set off all the dogs in the backyards; they barked loudly as if in a chorus line. The neighbours were banging and shouting from their windows for the dogs and the kids to shut up. The boys thought this was very funny, but they were just excited and in high spirits.

I fell asleep on the settee and Mum and Ann spent the whole morning chatting and drinking endless cups of tea. I eventually woke up but just laid there with my eyes closed listening to Mum's and Ann's voices droning on. The boys were still playing in the back yard.

'The Old Girl is going to go mad when she finds out Billy has got married,' said Mum.

'Well, it is her own fault,' Ann snapped, who never had got on with her mother. 'When Billy went to London with Shirley to meet her she called Shirley a big plonk, out to catch her boy for a meal ticket and also that she had a Manchester codswallop face and ate nothing but stinking tripe and onions. What does the Old Girl expect? Of course they wouldn't invite her, would they?'

'No, but I don't want to be around when she finds out. God knows what she will call her now.'

We shared pie and chips from the chip shop in the evening. Uncle Tony, who had a few fingers missing from one of his hands, was pleased to see us but after eating he couldn't wait to go to the pub to leave us all to get on with it. Ann, Mum and I shared the double bed whilst Joyce slept on a bed that was made up on cushions on the floor and the boys slept top and tail in Paul's bed. The settee was made up for Tony.

'I hope Tony remembers where he is sleeping when he comes home as he is bound to have had too many bevies,' said Ann as we climbed into bed. 'Do you know, he was forever coming home drunk at the weekends; he would get into bed then roll over to the edge and pee on the floor. He was too lazy and drunk to get up to go to the toilet and he expected me to clean it up in the morning. But I cured him, though, as I laid out his best suit next to the bed and he pissed all over it. He was furious next morning and we had a

129

big row, but I warned him I would do it again if he did not go to the toilet before he got into bed.'

Mum and I laughed at this story. It was not long before they were both asleep but I was so uncomfortable. There was hardly any room and the snoring from them was horrendous and pins and needles were running from my fingers tips up my arm.

Next morning we went by bus to Urmston, a posh part of Manchester, where Shirley lived with her mother. We met Billy and Shirley in the registry office. Billy wore his ill-fitting grey suit and Shirley wore a flowery suit with a matching-coloured felt hat. I stood next to the children in my new turquoise jacket, oatmeal-coloured tweed skirt and coffee-coloured blouse. Mum wore the same coat she had travelled in over her dress and cardigan and a small hat. Just before Billy slipped the ring on Shirley's finger he quickly glanced over her shoulder at me. I had no idea what he thought at that moment and I did not care either; I just hoped that he would stay in Manchester for good now. After we had had sandwiches, tea and Victoria sponge cake at the family's house we had to go.

Ann took us to Piccadilly, in the centre of Manchester, to look at the shops. We were to go home on the Monday evening, which could not come too soon for me as I wanted to go back to London. I did not like Manchester or being with Aunty Ann, as she had made a few unkind sarcastic remarks to me, though I chose to ignore them. I was sure she resented me for being Mum's daughter. Sunday we did not do much apart from taking the children to the park. Sharing a bed with Mum and Ann was so uncomfortable that I hardly had any sleep, so Monday morning I stayed in bed after Mum and Ann had gone downstairs. About eleven o'clock I got up and washed and dressed. Just as I had gone back into the bed-room Aunty Ann came bursting in and shouted at me, saying that I was a 'lazy cow' and why wasn't I downstairs helping my mother? I mumbled under my breath for her to shut up.

'What did you say?'

I picked up my handbag and coat and walked out of the bedroom to the top of the stairs.

'Don't you walk away from me when I asked you what you said?' Ann tugged at my jacket and swung me around. I pulled away from her but she thumped me around the head. 'You bitch!' she shouted, pulling at my hair.

'Leave me alone. I have done nothing to you.' I cried, trying to push her away.

In the struggle I lost my footing and slid down the narrow stairs on my back. only stopping my fall by grabbing the handrail. I stood up. My back and head hurt; I was shocked by Ann's outburst. I dashed the rest of the way down the stairs. Mum came into the lobby just as I opened the front door and fled. Mum was calling after me to come back, but with tears flowing I just wanted to be away from the nasty jealous cow. I was shaking like a jelly as I began the long walk, in my high heels, to Manchester city centre. I spent the rest of the day wandering around the shops, which were closed as it was Easter Monday. In the evening I made my way to the coach station. I went into the café next door and ordered a cup of tea and a bun. I felt sick and faint, as I had not eaten all day. A few seedy-looking men passed by the window. I turned away when they beckoned me to go with them. I felt and looked awful; I must have looked like a down-and-out.

I saw Mum and the children coming along the street followed by Aunty Ann.

'See, I told you she would be here, didn't I?' Ann said to Mum.

The coach was waiting and without a word I climbed on and took my seat. Mum and Ann said their goodbyes. I just thought good riddance to her and to Manchester.

Mum sat in the seat behind me and she settled the boys and Joyce down next to me. When they were asleep she asked me in a whisper whether I would like a slice of bread and cheese and that Ann had not meant to upset me. I did not reply. I thought that was *just* what Ann had intended to do; she was spiteful and nasty. I hated her and her jealous manipulative ways and she could stick Manchester where the sun doesn't shine. The coach journey seemed even longer going home and I was again feeling ill and faint by the bumping and rocking of the coach. I never wanted to go to Manchester again or to ever travel a long distance by coach.

I closed my eyes and thought about John. I had been snappy with him a few times recently so I promised myself I would be kinder in future. I now realized the reason I had been offhand was because I was always so tired. As I was drifting in and out of sleep, I thought about telling John I only wanted to see him at the weekends, as it was getting too much during the week after working all day.

When we arrived back in London I helped Mum with Joyce, the boys and the pushchair. After all, I thought, it was not Mum's fault that she had such a spiteful sister.

Chapter 22

I tried to ask John nicely if we could only see each other at the weekends for a few weeks, as I was feeling so tired during the week after working in the factory all day, but he became annoyed and asked if I had met anyone else. I said 'no' – it was just that I was constantly tired and needed to go to bed earlier, but I don't think he understood. One Friday evening, when Mum had taken the kids to the pictures and Dad was as usual at the club, John knocked at the door. He followed me in and I sat on the bottom of the stairs.

'What's the matter, Rose? Why aren't you ready to go out?' We were supposed to be going to see John's cousin and her husband and two boys who lived in Cricklewood.

'I don't want to go,' I said, picking at the sleeve of the cardigan John had bought me at Christmas.

He sat down beside me. 'Come on, Rose; we have to be there soon they are expecting us.'

'I don't want to go,' I repeated. 'I am too tired to go anywhere.'

There had never been a bulb in the light fitting along the passageway, so the only light was the light from the lamp post outside the house. We could barely see each other's faces. 'What's this all about, Rose?'

'I really don't want to go out, and here take this.' I handed him the small box containing my engagement ring. I had thought all day about giving the ring back and ending our relationship. It was going to be hard to break with John as he was a really nice person and I would miss him, but it was what I wanted. I could not cope anymore with working all day then getting ready to go out with John in the evenings. It was all too much for me and it was making me feel ill.

Taking the box, John said, 'What's this for?'

'It's over. I'm sorry but I don't want to be tied down any more. I don't think it's right when I can't get enthusiastic about seeing you, and I have tried to tell you I'm too tired to go out during the weekdays.'

'I see,' he said, twisting the box in his fingers. He was quiet for a while before saying. 'If I do accept this ring back and leave this house, that's it - you will never see me again.'

'I know, John, so just go,' I replied.

John turned and walked to the door. He paused and glanced around for a moment, his hand on the catch, but he could see that there was no changing my mind. He opened the door and slammed it hard behind him. The bang seemed to go right through me. I put my head on the stairs and my tears began to fall. Although I was upset, I also felt relieved, as I could not cope with any more pressure.

Mum was surprised when I told her next day that John and I had split up.

'But why?' she asked. 'I thought you two were good together.'

'Well, it's over now,' I said flippantly. 'I didn't want to be with John anymore. Besides there are many more fish in the sea.'

But I was only kidding myself. I did not want anyone else. I just could not be bothered anymore. I spent the next few weeks just going to work and coming home to bed, pleased I didn't have the hassle of getting ready to go out. And that suited me fine. Mum asked me one day when she brought me in a cup of tea and a sandwich, why I never went out in the evenings like I used to instead of keep shutting myself away in the bedroom. I just replied that I didn't feel like it after working all day. I knew Mum was worried about me but I assured her I was fine.

One Saturday, about six or seven weeks later, Mum was out shopping. I did my washing in the scullery and put the clothes into a bowl and went through the sitting room to go out the door leading to the garden. Dad, pencil in hand, had his football coupon spread out on the table, checking the results on the wireless. As I passed, with the bowl under my arm, the room seemed to suddenly change colour and began to spin. I turned to go back but fainted. I lay there too weak to move and drifted in and out of consciousness, but could still hear the commentator's voice, from the wireless, giving the sports results. Dad carried on checking his coupon and did not come to my aid at all; the most important thing to him was if he had won any money from the 'pools'. Next thing I remember was Mum trying to push the door open as I lay behind it. She bent over me.

'What's the matter, Rosie? How did you fall? Did you fall over the kids' toys or something?'

'No, Mum,' I said, struggling to my feet, 'I just felt a bit faint with the heat and besides I have not eaten today. I will be all right once I've had a cup of tea.'

Mum turned on Dad. 'How could you leave her there like that when she's hit her head and passed out. You bloody, stupid, idiot! The only thing you can think about is your bloody football results and what time the club opens. She could have cracked her head open for all you cared.'

I had a bump on the side of my head where I had knocked it when I fell.

Dad rose from his chair. Without saying a word, but eyes blazing behind his brown-rimmed glasses, he screwed his coupon up, threw it across the room and stormed out.

Mum made me a cup of tea and said I must have fallen over the shoes Kenny had left on the floor. I assured her I would feel better after I had had a lie-down.

The following weeks became much warmer and the people in the factory were sweltering. On one of these days I was making up boxes and filling them with bottles of hair tonic. I was finding it all too much for me – the heat, the constant bending, lifting and carrying, so after a cup of orange juice in the works canteen at lunchtime I walked out and got the bus home.

I tried to walk in a straight line when I got off the bus but it was difficult. I opened my legs to walk, not caring if people stared as I hobbled along looking as if I had wet myself. I could feel the perspiration trickling down my face. I knew without looking in a mirror that my face was as red as a beetroot. I just hoped Mum was not at home. I put my hand through the letter box to retrieve the front door key hanging on a piece of string and let myself in and tried to go quietly up the stairs towards my bedroom.

I heard Mum's voice from the back room. 'Is that you, Rosie?'

'Yes, Mum,' I called back over the banister, trying to sound as normal as possible. 'I'll be down soon,' I lied. 'We were all sent home early as the factory was too hot to work in.'

Once in my bedroom I took off my briefs then searched for a needle in my dressing table. I lay on the bed with my legs apart. My fingers found the large angry abscess that burned like a volcano in my inner thigh near to my groin. I raised my hand and stabbed with the needle into the centre. The sticky ooze trickled out onto my fingers but not enough to stop the pain. I stabbed again, then again, and squeezed the large angry lump until the poison ran freely of its own accord. I took a breather, then squeezed again and dug around with the needle to pick out the core. It began to bleed. I thought I was going to pass out. After a while I went to the bathroom and splashed my face with cold water, then put a wet flannel over the hole in my leg.

I heard mum call, 'Are you coming down, Rosie?'

Taking a deep breath, I called back, 'Yes soon. I just have a few things to do first.'

I went back to my bedroom and collapsed onto my bed, relieved that the poison was now out and I could begin to heal. It never occurred to me to see a doctor. I had only seen a doctor once before and could still remember the intrusive examination he had given me.

Next morning, although I still felt as if I was running a temperature, I went to work as normal. After I had clocked in and put on my white overall and hat, the supervisor came up to me and said I had to go to see the personnel officer at once. My heart skipped a beat as I nervously knocked on her door. I heard her say 'Come in!', I went in and she beckoned me to stand in front of her desk.

'I understand you went home at lunchtime yesterday without telling anyone that you were going.' She was a thin, dark-haired, poker-faced woman in her late thirties. She had a reputation for being very strict with all of the workers.

'I am sorry, Miss, but I did not feel well yesterday.'

'So why did you not tell anyone? What was the matter with you?'

'I felt bilious, Miss. I am sorry.'

'Not sorry enough to have let us know. You left us without anyone to cover the work. You can now leave the factory and not come back. You are sacked and your cards will be forwarded on to you.'

Shocked, I turned towards the door; it seemed far away. I tried to reach for the handle but could not quite get there. I fell to the floor. Next thing I remember is the factory first-aid nurse handing me a glass of water. The personnel officer helped me onto a chair. She knelt down beside me. 'Is there something you want to tell me, Rose?'

'I'm sorry,' I mumbled. 'I really was not well yesterday.'

'I realize that, Rose. Like I said, is there something you would like to tell me?'

I did not answer but just looked into the glass of water.

'Well!' she probed.

'I'm having a baby,' I said very quietly. It was the first time I had even admitted this to myself.

'I thought you were, Rose. Do your parents know about this?'

'No!' I cried. 'My Dad would kill me if he knew.'

'Well, it's something you can't keep secret for long, is it? They will have to know sooner or later. Surely they must have noticed you were showing signs of pregnancy.'

The sobs were now coming uncontrollable from my very being. I could hardly catch my breath. I just wanted the floor to swallow me up.

'Does your boyfriend know about this?'

'I don't have a boyfriend,' I replied in between the sobs.

'I see,' she said. 'Where does your father work?'

'The Crypto.'

'My husband is the manager there. I will phone him and ask him to inform your father.'

'No!' I sobbed even louder. 'Please don't tell him.'

'Well, he has to know,' she said firmly. 'Go and get your things while I call him, then I will take you home so we can tell your mother.'

The girls on the factory floor saw me leaving the office and began to whisper to each other as I passed. I felt so ashamed and tried to hide my bloated face. What will happen to me now? I thought, and what will Dad do? When I was ready the woman escorted me to her car and drove me home.

Mum looked surprised at seeing the two of us on the doorstep. 'What on earth is the matter?' she asked anxiously.

'Can I come in?'

Mum never let people into the house so she said that she could step just inside the passageway.

'There is no other way to tell you this, Mrs Handleigh, but your daughter is pregnant.'

'What?' Mum turned angrily to me 'Get up those stairs right now,' she said, pointing towards the stairs. 'I'll deal with you later.'

The personnel lady put her hand on my arm. 'Go on,' she said 'It will be all right, you'll see. Have tomorrow off and I will see you as normal at work on Monday morning.'

I rushed to my room and left them to it. I was dreading Dad coming home, not knowing what he would do. I just didn't know what to think any more. My head hurt and my body felt as if it was on fire.

Mum came into my bedroom ranting, 'How long did you think you could hide this from us? You'd think you would know better than to have sex at your age after all the fuss last year with Tony. I gather this is John's baby, isn't it?'

'Of course it is,' I said.

'Did you think you could get away with this? You are only fifteen, Rosie. What will the neighbours say now when this gets around? How could you bring all this shame on us? Your Dad says you are as rotten as an apple and I am beginning to believe him. How could you have done this to us?'

I was all cried out by now and my head felt as if it was overloaded. I couldn't take much more; I just wanted to sleep. I put my head in my hands then lay down on the bed. Mum left the room, still ranting that she did not know what my father would do when he got home.

My heart skipped a beat when I heard Dad come in. Mum had been waiting at the door. 'Where is that bitch?' he shouted.

'She's in her room.' Mum barred his way as he tried to climb up the stairs.

'No, Norman. Leave her alone. We have to sort this out.'

'Get out of my way!' He tried to push pass her.

Mum stood her ground. 'I said no and I mean it. You will not touch her.'

Dad stepped back. 'I'm telling you, woman: I want her out of here and gone before the whole street knows she is having a kid. She's out of here. I told you all along she was no good.'

I heard his footsteps along the passage going towards the room at the back of the house and then the door slamming. I sighed with relief. I could not bear to face him right now. I fell into a deep sleep.

Later Mum came into my room with a cup of tea and two slices of bread and jam.

'Here, Rosie,' she said softly. 'Have this – you will feel better.'

I sat up, realizing I had not eaten all day.

'Thank you,' I whispered, taking the cup and plate from her. 'I'm so sorry, Mum.'

'I expect you are but try not to worry too much for now,' she said. 'What's done is done.'

Mum sat beside me on the bed. 'Social services have been informed and so have the police. We have to report to the police station and social services tomorrow morning.'

'Oh no, Mum!' I cried. 'Not the police. I don't want to go to the police.' I dreaded being locked up in a police cell again.

'You have no choice, Rosie. You are underage and it's against the law for you to have sex, so of course they will have to be seen. The personnel woman phoned the social services; she had a duty to do so.'

Just when I thought I could no longer cry, a tear escaped and fell into the teacup.

Chapter 23

Sitting on a hard spindly wooden chair in the small waiting room, I studied the hands and black Roman numbers on the large wooden clock that hung on the wall opposite. I tried to take my mind off of what was going on in the next room. The ticking seemed louder and echoed around the almost empty room. It had been thirty minutes since Mum had gone in to speak to the social worker. My instinct was to run away, but where could I run to and what could I do, me, fifteen years old and pregnant? I watched the hand of the clock move to the next minute, Mum had been so long in there and I was now getting annoyed. It's me they're discussing, I thought, and I should be in there, too. I put my hands to my ears in frustration, trying to drown out the tick-tock tick-tock. After what seemed ages, the door opened and Mum came out, accompanied by a woman in a charcoal-grey suit who asked Mum to wait while she saw to me. The woman beckoned me to go into her room and she followed me in. 'Sit down, please,' she said curtly. Her thick straight grey hair was cut to her ears, which made her face seem longer than it was.

I sat on the chair the other side of her desk. 'Now, Rose,' she said, sitting facing me. I thought she had a false smile and I didn't trust her. 'I have spoken to your mother at some length and we have reached a decision as to what to do about your predicament.'

I concentrated on the pain where the abscess had been. It still hurt and I was thinking that I really had to buy some ointment for it when I got the chance.

'Are you listening to me?'

I tried to pay attention. 'Yes,' I replied.

'On Monday you are to go back to work as normal,' she continued. 'I have spoken to Personnel and you will have to leave work at twelve o'clock next Friday and go home and wait for me to call and collect you.' She looked to see if this was getting through to me as I must have looked blank. 'I will be taking you to a hostel in Richmond until I can find a mother and baby home for you to go to. How far gone are you?'

'I don't know,' I replied quietly.

'When was your last period?'

I thought for a while, trying to remember, and then replied that it was most probably in January.

'That's makes you almost five months. How your mother hadn't noticed is beyond me.'

I did not reply. How dare she criticize my mother? It was not her fault.

'As I said,' she repeated, noticing my look of anger, 'you will be going to a hostel in Richmond until I can find the mother and baby home for you to go to. Once you have the baby it will be put up for adoption and you can then get on with your life as if nothing has happened. You do want the baby adopted, don't you?'

I had not thought that far ahead so just nodded.

She rose from her chair. 'Well, that's all I have to say for now, apart from to tell you to make sure you are ready on Friday. Your mother is now going to take you to the police station, which is the normal procedure as you are underage.' She escorted me to the door to join my mother.

'Do make sure Rose is ready on Friday,' she said to Mum as we left.

We went on the trolleybus back to Harlesden. We did not speak until we were off the bus and near to the police station.

Mum was irritable. 'This all serves you right, Rosie,' she said crossly, hurrying along as I walked one step behind her. 'Why on earth didn't you learn your lesson after last year? I warned you not to do bad things again and now look at all the trouble you have caused. What the neighbours are going to say now if this all gets out doesn't bear thinking about.'

We went through the wooden doors at the police station. At the desk Mum asked to see the person who was expecting us. I was so nervous I began to tremble and my teeth and chin would not stop chattering. We sat down to wait. After a while a door opened at the side of the main desk and a policeman asked me to come in. Mum got up to follow but was asked to wait where she was. I was shown into a small office and told to be seated until the person seeing me was free. I looked around the chilly room at the grey metal cabinets and read the police crime prevention posters on the wall. After what seemed ages for someone to come in to see me, the man in charge eventually entered. He was followed by another man who made himself busy by searching through the cabinets and reading the index cards. The tall, broad-shouldered detective in charge sat down, statement sheets in front of him, pen at the ready. His steely eyes behind his wire-framed glasses were fixed on me for a few moments, which I presume was to try to unnerve me. He wore a dark suit and blue shirt and tie; he had a thin dark moustache across his top lip.

'My name is Detective Maynard and I am here to discover the facts that led to you becoming pregnant.'

I wanted to be anywhere but there and wished the floor would swallow me up or for me to be transported to another galaxy. I studied the scratches on the wooden desk to take my mind off of the questions he was asking me, but all I could hear was his monotonous voice.

'What address does Mr John Kent live at? How old is he? How old are you? Did John Kent force his attentions on you? Were you a willing party? How often did you have intercourse? Where were you when you had intercourse? Did you remove your clothes or did he remove your clothes? Did he know how old you were?' Over and over the man bombarded me with questions. I was exhausted and I just wanted to go home. I did not answer any of his questions so he snatched up his papers and left the room in a huff.

The other man, who had been looking in the filing cabinets, came over to me and said kindly, 'You may as well answer the questions, Rose, or you will be here all night and your mum will want to get off home soon, so do yourself a favour – co-operate and then you can go.'

The other man returned and asked if I was ready to answer the questions yet. I said I was. I answered the questions with a 'yes' or 'no'. When it was all over the man asked me to read and sign at the bottom of the page. I was shocked to see he had written the statement as though I had said the whole sentences that were his questions and not the 'yes' or 'no' I had said to him. I was upset – it did not seem right to me the statement being written in such a cold calculating way. I wanted to say that that is not how it happened; it was not like that at all. But I didn't; I just wanted get out of there as soon as possible. I sniffed and swallowed back the tears as I signed the statement. I did not want this pig of a man to see me cry; I just wanted to go home. I was emotionally drained, feeling faint and my head felt like a heavy boulder.

The following week went by in a haze. I returned to work and had to report to the personnel woman to confirm that I would be leaving on Friday. She kindly told me that, after I had had the baby and it had been adopted, I could come back to work there as if nothing had happened. I thanked her and she said I would be working in the powdered shampoo section until Friday, as it was a sitting-down job. I could feel the other workers' eyes studying me as I walked past them. The shampoo room was partitioned off by a glass screen and on the other side were two men who worked the machine that tipped the powder into paper envelopes. Then the envelopes were shuffled through a hole in the glass to be packed by the women into boxes. I could not stop sneezing while I was in there and my eyes felt heavy and watered as if I had a cold, so I was given a cotton mask to wear. At break time I sat on my own. I was ostracized and conscious of the nudging and whispers between the factory workers. Even girls I had been friendly with daren't talk to me now. On the Wednesday during the tea break, an older woman named Rita sidled up to me and quietly said that she knew someone who could help me for a price, but only if I could keep my mouth shut. I looked horrified at her and ran back to my work place. It was obvious that I was being talked about and it was also obvious that I was being shunned as no one wanted to be near me, but I wasn't worried as then, at least, they could not ask me awkward questions.

At home, Mum asked me to go into my bedroom each evening before Dad returned home from work, so as not to wind him up. On the evening before I was leaving I sat on my bed looking out of the window. It was raining heavily and I watched the rain fairies dancing on the pathway. I had never felt so lonely or alone.

Mum had come into my bedroom earlier and said she had heard from the police that John had denied everything. 'He has said you had finished with him as you had met someone else when you were in Manchester and whoever it was must be the father.'

'That's such a lie, Mum,' I replied angrily. 'You know I didn't meet anyone else in Manchester and, besides, I was already about two or three months pregnant then. John is the

145

father and he knows it. He just doesn't want to go to prison or be deported, so he would say that, wouldn't he?' I was so upset that he was denying he was the father of this baby. How dare he do that!

'I know,' said Mum, 'but you can't blame him wanting to save his own skin.'

I had packed my bag ready to leave the following day. I had two smocks and two skirts that Mum had bought for me in C&A's in Oxford Street the previous Saturday. I also packed a bar of soap, flannel, underwear and a hairbrush. Now I was all ready to leave my home. The rain beat down and I shed a tear. How had I been so stupid and how could I have trusted someone again? How dare John accuse me of meeting someone else? I am such a fool. I cried tears of frustration, not only because of my situation but also out of fear as to what would happen to me. I was being banished from my home and also leaving behind my little sister Joyce. She always came running to me for a cuddle when she saw me – would she miss me as much as I would miss her?

At one thirty on the Friday the social worker arrived to take me to Richmond. Mum stood alone on the doorstep as I went. She did not say a word of goodbye and did not make eye contact with me. She just stood there with her arms crossed. I could not help thinking she was glad to see the back of me and I hated my father for chucking me out. The social worker, Miss Davis, and I arrived at a large corner house at the top of a hill, not far from Richmond Park. I was left in the hands of a middle-aged woman, Miss Holden. Miss Davis said as she was leaving that she would be in touch when a mother and baby home could be found for me to go to. Miss Holden showed me upstairs to a room containing two beds and a chest of drawers.

'You will be sharing with another girl named Pat,' said Miss Holden. 'She should be back from work in a while. As soon as you have unpacked, come and join me downstairs.'

I stood for a few moments, taking in the very basic furniture, one chest of drawers and a single wardrobe. I unpacked my few things and went downstairs. I tiptoed along the hallway wondering exactly what room Miss Holden was in. I found her sitting at a table in the kitchen peeling potatoes; there was also a pile of runner beans waiting to be done.

'Oh, there you are! Come and sit down and I will explain a few things to you.' She put the peeler down, then pushed her large, clear plastic glasses further up the bridge of her nose. 'On Monday you will be starting work at 9 a.m. in a photographer's shop in the High Street. You will leave work at 5.30 p.m., then you will return straight back here and help to prepare the evening meal. Every morning before work you will air your bed and after breakfast at 7 a.m. you will go back to the bedroom to make your bed. On pay day, which will be on Fridays, you will pay me for your keep. On Saturdays you are expected to spend the day cleaning the house from top to bottom and helping as necessary to prepare the daytime and evening meals. You will spend Sundays quietly doing your own chores – for instance ironing your clothes ready for work.' Miss Holden handed me a small kitchen knife. 'Here, you can now help prepare this evening's dinner.'

I felt stupid when Miss Holden had to show me how to cut the runner beans. The smell of them nauseated me and there seemed so many of them to get through; I was beginning to think there must be an army of people living here. As it turned out, there were only four girls and two staff. I shared a room with Pat, a girl of about nineteen. She had been involved with a married man who left her when she became pregnant. I did not want to talk much to anyone else, either in the house or at the photographer's. I had become very withdrawn; I was so unhappy being away from everything I had known.

The work in the photographer's shop was easy, as I just had to help with the picture developing in the dark room. I put the negatives in one solution tray then transferred them into another solution and then hung them up with pegs. I also cut the edge of the photographs and put them into envelopes ready for customers to collect. There was just a man and a women working in the shop and I was pleased that they did not ask me any awkward questions.

A few days later I had to visit the local doctor's surgery to see a nurse for an antenatal check-up. She dug about on my stomach, digging her fingers this way and that, before putting what looked like a silver eggcup to her ear, and pressed the other end down on me for her to hear the baby's heartbeat. The nurse said everything was fine with me and the baby. The baby moved about and kicked quite a lot, but I did not feel emotionally connected, as I knew the baby was not going to be mine; it would be given away to strangers, to people that would be able to take good care of him or her.

At the beginning of August, Miss Holden informed me the social worker, Miss Davis, was coming to take me to a mother and baby home the other side of London and I was to be ready when she came. I started to cry when Miss Holden told me this, but I don't know why. I suppose it was my hormones. I was missing my mum and feeling cast out and unwanted by anyone.

Thursday, 9 August 1956 – my sixteenth birthday. This was the day that was supposed to change my life. The day Tony was going to come back for me. It was the day John and I were going to plan our wedding day after breaking the news of our engagement to our families. Instead, I was being escorted by a social worker from a Richmond hostel to a mother and baby home in Grove Park on the other side of London, a place I had never heard of. There were no birthday cards, no presents, no one to wish me a happy birthday, no friends, no family. I felt so miserable and alone.

Miss Davis sat beside me on the train and asked me if I was feeling all right. I thought 'What a stupid question!' but replied 'Yes'. I looked at my reflection in the train window. I did not look all right; in fact, I looked sick, a thin-faced stranger with dark lines under my tired eyes and not at all how a sixteen-year-old girl was supposed to look.

'You will be all right in the mother and baby home,' she assured me. 'It's run by the Church Army and they will take good care of you until after the baby is born. Try not to look so worried.'

'It's my birthday today,' I whispered. I just wanted someone to say 'Happy birthday'. But the social worker did not hear me over the sound of the train engine.

We arrived at Grove Park station and walked for about ten minutes until we came to a large detached house, set back from the road.

'Here we are,' said Miss Davis.

I carried my small suitcase slowly up the gravel path to the front door. Miss Davis rang the brass doorbell. The door was answered by a lady dressed in a grey cotton uniform. She had a matching grey headscarf tied under her brown hair at the back. Her face looked as if it had been scrubbed with a brush, it was so red and shiny. She wore black lace-up shoes and black stockings.

'Come in,' she said politely. As we entered, I could smell a combination of lavender polish and pine disinfectant. The hallway was wide and had highly polished blue-and-green, paisley-patterned linoleum flooring that also went up the wide stairway.

The woman in grey, who I found out later was the matron, said to me, 'Rose, leave your case here in the hallway and go into that room there, whilst I have a word with Miss Davis in the staffroom.'

I opened the door to a very large room and came face to face with about twenty girls sitting around two long tables. A hush went around the room as if they had stopped talking when I entered and all eyes were on me. A lady, also in a grey uniform, rose from a dining chair, clapped her hands and said, 'As you were, girls,' then asked me to sit down beside her at the table. 'It is afternoon teatime now and I expect you are hungry, so help yourself to a cup of tea, a sandwich and a piece of cake,' she said.

I thanked her and nervously stood to pour the tea from a large, silver teapot into a white tea cup. I was conscious of the girls still looking at me, my hands were shaking and I missed the cup and some of the tea slopped into the saucer. I sat down and added sugar and milk to the tea. There were sandwiches and fruit cake on the table but I did not feel hungry. A girl in a red smock, sitting the other side of the table, placed a sandwich and a piece of cake onto my plate. 'Eat up!' she said quietly to me. 'Supper is not until six thirty and even if you're not feeling hungry your baby certainly will be.' I felt the baby move and thought she must be right so I ate a little.

Everyone was talking quietly again. I glanced around the tables. None of the girls looked much more than eighteen, and some looked as if they should be in junior school. I could not tell who was pregnant and who wasn't, as all were dressed in different-coloured smock tops. The other side of the room had numerous armchairs and the grey-coloured walls had cracks, some running from floor to ceiling. Some were quite wide, so that it looked, in places, like a road map. All the cracks had dates written in pencil next to it. A girl saw me looking at the wall and said that the house was con-demned and the dates were when the cracks had first appeared.

'What's your name?' said the girl. I told her my name just as the sound of a baby could be heard crying from somewhere in the house. The girl who had given me the sandwich said to another girl, 'Oh no, that's your baby crying, Susan, and he will now wake all the others up.' True to her word the sound of other babies could be heard crying. Three of the girls asked the woman in grey if they could leave the room to see to their babies.

I was relieved when the matron opened the door and told me to come and say goodbye to Miss Davis. 'I will see you again a few weeks after the baby's born. So goodbye for now.' She shook hands with the matron and hurried off out of the front door.

Matron turned to me. 'Pick your case up, Rose, and follow me. I will show you to your room.'

I followed her up the stairs and into a dormitory containing four neatly made-up beds one side and three beds on the opposite side.

She walked over to a bed. 'This dormitory is called the Blue Room; it's where you will be sleeping. We also have a Yellow Room and a Green Room.' She pointed to a door in the corner. 'In that room are the wardrobes that you will be sharing with the other girls and also two washbasins'

I put down my suitcase beside a blue-painted bedside locker that had three small jars on top. The matron picked them up one by one. 'This jar contains nipple cream; you are to rub this onto your nipples twice a day to stop them from cracking.' She picked the next one up. 'This jar is for stretch marks. You will also rub this on twice a day. This last jar, with the spatula, is for you to put a sample in and hand it to the nurse for it to go away to be analysed, to make sure you don't have dysentery.' She turned to go. 'I will leave you to unpack, then come downstairs and I will let you know the rules of this house.'

When she had gone I sat on the bed and a tear from each eye silently rolled down my cheek and fell onto my hand. I took the hankie I had put up my sleeve and wiped the tears away.

Chapter 24

I was perspiring so much the sweat was dripping from my face onto the stairs. I ran the cloth over the lino again and put the bucket of warm soapy water down another step. This was my duty for today, to clean the landing, stairs and hallway. It seemed to be never ending and by now I hated the sight of the paisley-patterned flooring. Matron had informed me the previous evening of all the rules of the house – the list seemed to go on forever. All the dos and don'ts – it was all so regimental. No wonder they named themselves 'The Church Army'.

Every morning we were to strip our beds, then go to breakfast. Afterwards we were to go back and make our beds, then stand beside the bed until Sister or Matron checked to see that it was made correctly. We were then to go into the musky, corrugated building next door to the house, for morning prayer and worship. After this we were to look on the noticeboard in the dining room to see what our duty was for that day. On my first day this was to clean the landing, stairs and hallway. My tummy was now getting quite big and it was an effort to bend down to wash the lino. Feeling hot and faint, I stopped to rest by sitting on the stairs beside the bucket of soapy water.

Suddenly there was a commotion in the hallway

downstairs. Looking through the stair rails, I could see a girl screaming and struggling with a man and a woman, who I presumed were her parents. She was trying to reach out for her baby, which the matron had taken from her arms.

'Shane, Shane, I love you. My baby! Let me go! I want my baby!'

The matron pulled back and without saying a word rushed into the nursery with the baby and kicked the door shut. The girl was still struggling and screaming like an injured animal.

'Please, Mum; if you love me, you would let me keep my baby,' the girl cried.

Her mother clung to her. 'It's because we *do* love you that the baby has to go.'

The man picked up the girl's suitcase and said in a stern voice, 'You know this is for the best. Come on, it's time to go home.'

The girl was led out of the front door by her parents, still sobbing her heart out.

I cleaned the next few stairs, then I saw Matron answer the door to a very nervous-looking, well-dressed couple. She led them into the staffroom and after about five minutes they emerged again. Sister came out of the nursery with the baby in her arms.

'Here he is,' said Matron, taking the baby and handing it over to the lady. 'He is a little beauty.'

I sighed, wiped my forehead with the back of my hand and shook my head.

The couple were overwhelmed; they looked so happy. 'Oh! He is lovely. More than I ever imagined him to be.' The lady put her finger into the sleeping baby's little fist.

Sister handed a suitcase to the man. 'There is everything you will need for the baby, including his bottles and feed. He has not long been fed so he will be sleeping until you arrive home.'

'Thank you so much,' replied the lady. 'I just can't thank

you enough for all you have done. We are so happy and we love him already.'

They said their goodbyes and were gone.

I was amazed by what I had witnessed. One person's sorrow was another person's joy.

I felt my baby kick as I continued to wash the stairs. I will not cry at all, I thought, when my baby goes. It's for the best – after all, what could I offer the baby? Nothing at all. Nix, naught, nothing, as my mother would say. And why? Because I had nothing, not even my own family or a home to go to. I was becoming so choked up – what was going to become of me? Where was I going to go when I eventually had to leave? Would my dad let me go home? I doubted it, as I had caused so much trouble and I supposed he must have chucked me out for good. I just did not know any of the answers.

Eventually I finished my duty and emptied the bucket of soapy water into the drain in the back garden and went up to the Blue Room and collapsed on the bed. Millie, the girl who had the bed next to mine, came in and crashed out on her bed.

'Oh I am so tired. I have been swinging that bumper over the floor for ages,' she said. Millie had short dark hair and was very slim apart from the belly bulge in the front; she had a sharp, but pleasant face with a prominent Roman nose. 'Did you hear that girl when she left her baby?'

'Yes,' I replied. 'It was awful. Everyone must have heard all the commotion.'

'I know it is but you do get used to it. Almost every week when someone leaves it's the same thing. It's best in the long run for the baby.'

I could not help but feel this was a case of brainwashing by everyone concerned.

I tried to turn on my side but gave up and lay on my back again. 'I just hope my baby goes to a really rich family that can give it everything I can't.'

'Yeah, and me,' Millie said, getting up from the bed. 'I'm just going to have a wash before lunchtime. By the way there is a new girl arriving later on and she will have that bed over there.'

It was really astonishing that there were so many girls in the same predicament as me. I had thought that I was the only one that was an underage pregnant girl. There were so many and this place was just like a baby factory.

I joined Millie at the sink and stripped down to the waist for a wash-down. 'That little girl, Averill, in the corner bed, is only twelve years old,' said Millie. 'Apparently she was sitting on her doorstep waiting for her mother to come home and a man grabbed her, dragged her behind the bushes and raped her.'

'Poor little mite,' I replied, 'and so young, just a baby herself. What happened to you, Millie?'

'I had a Turkish Cypriot boyfriend who made me pregnant and then hopped it. Don't know where he is, but to be fair, we did split up before I knew I was having a baby.'

'Millie, that's almost what happened to me!' I gasped. 'Only my boyfriend was an Armenian Cypriot.'

'Well, I never. That's odd,' said Millie. 'Only trouble is, Rose, that our babies will not be blond-haired and blue-eyed so it may be more difficult to find them adoptive parents.'

I had not thought of this. Although John had black hair and brown eyes, he was not dark skinned so surely a childless couple would want him or her, whatever colour the eyes.

Jane, another girl from our dormitory, came in and heard the end of our discussion. 'Yes, haven't you noticed there are no foreign girls here and that no one here is having a half-caste baby? They only want white babies.'

'That's awful,' I said, beginning to think that the babies were only being given to people who wanted a baby they could pass off as their own. Would these babies ever learn the truth of their birth when they grew up? Would they learn

155

how their mothers had loved them but had no option but to give them up?

We went for lunch with the other girls. Sister said that each day we were to move one seat along at the dining tables. The Sister sat at one end of the table and another Sister sat at the end of the other table. In the afternoons it was time to go to the dormitories for an hour's lie-down. The girls that had had their babies were to lay face down with a pillow under their stomach to help it to go back into place. Then it was afternoon tea. Those who were on mealtime duties had to help prepare the evening meal and the other girls could read or knit. After dinner we had to go back into the chapel for evening prayers. After prayers we had to line up outside Sister's first-aid room and we were each given a red pill for iron, a brown one for vitamins, a spoonful of cod-liver oil and, for those that were constipated, a spoonful of liquid paraffin. When it was time for me to have a spoonful of cod-liver oil, I heaved and ran to the toilet and was sick as a dog and I flatly refused to take any more ever again. Sister insisted, saying my body required it for the baby and I must take it. But the next evening when I was almost sick all over her floor, she could see that I just could not swallow the revolting stuff without bringing it and my dinner up, so I was excused.

On Fridays we had to go to the post office to receive our allowance money then to come back and line up outside the staffroom to hand over the money for our keep. We were handed back five shillings. I was told by Matron that I would receive a one-off payment from the government, which was a maternity grant, of about eight or nine pounds; it was to be spent on things needed for the baby. Matron gave me a list and said that it was compulsory for me to buy these things for the baby. They would be given to the new parents.

three vests
three winceyette nighties

156

three matinee jackets,
three dozen terry towelling nappies
three pairs of booties
three pairs of mittens
three baby's bonnets
three baby's feeding bottles
three teats
three tins of National Health baby's food
three bottles of National Health orange juice
one baby's shawl
two baby's blankets
three cot sheets
Johnson's baby cream and powder,
cotton wool.

'That's an awful lot to buy,' I whispered to Millie.

'Well, can you knit the woolly things yourself? It will keep the cost down.'

'I will have to. I will need wool, needles and patterns.'

I was thankful that my mum had taught me to knit and how to follow a pattern.

Chapter 25

After the lights were switched off, I lay in bed listening to the sound of crying from the new girl, who had arrived earlier that evening. I was passing in the hallway when she had arrived with her glamorous mother, who was dressed all in black, with lots of gold jewellery, and whiffed of expensive perfume. I recognized the mother as being a famous model from the adverts on the billboards and in the newspapers. The new girl's name was Helga. Although her name sounded foreign, she was English and seventeen years old, a year older than me, but seemed very much younger. Helga's crying soon set the little girl, Averill, crying, too, and then the other girls Millie, Jane, Diana and Jean joined in. To make matters worse, it was pouring with rain outside and flashes of lightning lit the room and the rumble of thunder sent us all hiding under the covers. Eventually the storm drifted into the distance and the rumbles of thunder grew fainter. The rain still lashed the windows but after a while it fell silent and a small voice whispered, 'Goodnight and God bless.' It was Helga. I softly said, 'Goodnight, Helga,' and fell fast asleep.

On Sundays, Millie, Jean and I were allowed to go to the church, which was about ten minutes' walk away from the house. I asked Helga if she would like to come with us and she said, yes, she would like to. We explained to Helga the only reason we went to church was because we were able to get out of doing heavy chores on Sunday mornings. We could see Helga was feeling very down and she was a little tearful, but she felt better by the time we arrived back at the house after the service. After Sunday dinner we helped clear the tables and then did the washing up so we did not get away with doing no work at all. Besides the morning and evening prayers in the chapel next to the house, the days seemed an endless round of chores – if it was not washing and polishing floors, or doing kitchen duties, it was doing washing in large butler sinks in the large wash house, a corrugated shed at the back of the house. In the wash house there were numerous gas boilers to boil sheets, towels and baby's nappies. The washing lines hung side by side outside the washroom and were always full, except on Sundays, when the washing was never done or hung out. The garden was very large and nicely kept by the sisters and a gardener, an old man who was a volunteer worker. There were a few trees, shrubs and flower beds surrounding the neat lawn. A flagstone veranda stretched the width of the house with a few tubs dotted about. On warm days the babies were placed in big bouncy prams with the bonnets up and netting across to keep flying insects out. The mothers were not allowed to wheel the babies or to pick them up; too much contact with the babies by the mothers was discouraged. The only contact the mothers were allowed with their babies was at bath and feed time. This was also the only time the mothers were allowed to enter the nursery unless they had permission to do so.

I attended for weekly antenatal check-ups in Lewisham Hospital, where I would be having my baby. We had to go in pairs to the hospital and to make our new appointments in the afternoons. We were to be back by four o clock or we would be in trouble with Matron. I usually attended the hospital with Millie as she would be having her baby there as well. Many of the girls were going to have their babies in Bromley Hospital.

The nurses and doctors, although they acted in a professional manner, made me feel very uncomfortable by their offhand attitude towards me. They did nothing to put me at ease, and I thought they treated me badly and I just wanted to say to them, 'Look here, my pregnancy has nothing to do with you; I'm only sixteen and scared of having this baby, so mind your own business and just do your job as you are meant to do.' But of course I said nothing, as their rude attitude was just something I would, in time, have to get used to. I asked Millie, Jane, Diane and Jean, when we were resting on our beds, if they were being treated badly at the hospital and whether they, too, felt that the people there were taking it upon themselves to sit in judgement upon us, or was it just my imagination.

'Of course they do,' said Jean. 'We are unmarried mothers-to-be and we are considered to have committed a dreadful sin and, in their eyes, we will be going to hell.'

'Yes,' said Diane, twisting her fingers around her blonde curls, 'that's right. We're not decent people like them. That's why they look down their noses.'

'They are afraid they will be contaminated by us,' added Millie, laughing.

'Well, in that case. Sod 'em,' I replied. 'It's none of their business.'

On the way back from the hospital I had bought a white shawl and wool and needles to knit a matinee jacket. These were the first things I had bought for the baby, and each evening I was busy knitting matinee jackets and bonnets. I tried to buy a little something for the baby every week and I would gently run my fingers lovingly over the baby clothes before folding them neatly in tissue paper and putting them into my bedside locker.

In September there was the Harvest Festival at the church and a mountain of fresh vegetables and fruit that had been donated by the church congregation was delivered to the house and we were all kept busy wrapping apples, pears, plums, potatoes, marrows and onions in newspaper to put into boxes for the winter. I enjoyed being in the kitchen, with the Sister who did the cooking, when it was my turn on the rota to help her. The kitchen had a cardinal-red stone-tiled floor, a large double oven with a cream-painted mantelpiece around it, and copper saucepans and colanders hanging up on big hooks. A wooden hanger hung from the ceiling with dried herbs and flowers tied to it. There was a large walk-in larder with shelves either side with all sorts of bottles, jars and white enamelled tins and containers holding all the kitchen provisions. The only thing I did not like whilst working in the kitchen was the mountain of washing up to be done after every meal. One day I became very dizzy in the heat of the kitchen so it was decided by Matron that I could no longer work in there in case I caused an accident, so I was returned to house-cleaning duties.

Towards the middle of September I received a letter from the personnel woman from the Vaseline factory asking me how I was, which I thought was very kind of her. I wrote back to say I was well and to ask whether, after the baby was born and sent for adoption, it would still be all right for me to return to my job at the factory. She wrote back a couple of days later and said that the offer of work still stood. This was a relief for me but I still had the problem of where I would be living if Dad would not let me return home. I became very melancholy after reading this letter, as it was a reminder of my family and everything I knew and just how much I missed them all. I put the letter down beside me on the bed and tried to hold back the tears that were threatening to overflow.

'Try not to get upset,' said little Averill. She cuddled her ragdoll close to her as she sat on her bed watching me studying the letter. Trying to inject reassurance into her voice she added, 'This is just a nightmare and it will soon pass and everything will be back to normal – you'll see.'

161

I swallowed back the tears, and thought this was typical of Averill to be such a sweet girl and she was so young to have to be going through all of this. She had shoulder-length straight dark hair with a straight fringe above her green eyes. She stroked her bump; it looked as if she was hiding a ball up her smock. Her ordeal was so much worse than mine and yet she tried to stay positive and I really admired her. What a nightmare for her and, under the circumstances, I thought she would surely be better off giving her baby up for adoption as it was the result of having been raped. Jean had told me that they had not caught the man that had raped Averill and she had told her that she hoped that they didn't, as she was terrified of going to court. I understood this as I too hoped that John had not been charged because if he had been I would have to go to court as well. I had made up my mind that if I did have to go to court I would tell them it was not rape and I had consented and John and I were engaged to be married. I doubted though that they would understand or believe someone as young as me, but I would tell them anyway. They would most probably make me feel stupid as they had made me feel when I had given a statement to the police. I had not heard from my mother or the social worker, so I assumed that the police would not take it any further and especially as I was now sixteen.

The girls in our dormitory were all due to have their babies around the same time. The other girls, in the Yellow Room, had almost all had their babies in the past few weeks and as they would leave, new girls would come in. The Green Room was much smaller and girls came and went there also. It seemed to me to be like a conveyer belt, pregnant girls in and out of the home, producing babies all the time for other people. The mothers were always so tearful after having had their babies; it was a mixture of 'postnatal blues' and knowing that they would soon be leaving to go back to their previous lives as if nothing had happened. I could not help thinking that, as every girl in the 'home' was under eighteen and therefore would be unlikely to be able to support a child on their own, it all must have been a deliberate ploy bringing them here. It was as if these babies were being stolen from their mothers to satisfy the needs of childless couples. But who was I to think or judge about all of this when I would have to give my baby away, too? Like them, I had nowhere to go and no means to keep a child.

One day one of the mothers from the Yellow Room whispered to me that she was going to go through the window after lights were out and asked if I wanted to go with her and a few of the others, who were fed up with being cooped up. She said they were going to go out for the night and would be back before anyone missed them. I replied, 'What would I want to go out for with a bump like this? And, besides, I'm too tired to go out gallivanting!' Anyway it turned out that this girl went out of the window on her own and got caught coming back through the window, a few hours later, by Sister. This girl was in big trouble. We were woken up by her screaming but there was nothing we could do to help her so we covered our heads to drown out the noise. The girl was never seen by us in the 'home' again. The matron asked us all to stand at breakfast time and she gave us a stern lecture about how this sort of behaviour would not be tolerated and that this should be a warning to us all. But we never did find out what happened to the girl or her baby. I was just relieved that I had not gone with her that night. About a couple of weeks later, another girl, named Betty, who was the same age as me, went into hospital to have her baby and we were told that she would not be returning as she had sadly lost her baby. Rumour was that the girl had died, too, which made all of us pregnant girls very worried; we just prayed that we would be all right.

I had witnessed many girls in floods of tears, leaving the home without their babies, and I was thinking again about the baby I was having. Would I really be able to give up my own flesh and blood? I tried to brush these feelings away but they kept coming to mind again and again; but I knew there was no way I could keep a baby. I had nowhere to live and how could I afford to support a baby? The thoughts would not go away; they went round and round in my head. Why couldn't I just shut off my thoughts until I left this place? It would be out of the question to keep a baby. I had no choice, just like all the other mothers that would be leaving here alone to live the rest of their lives with no one ever knowing they had had a baby. My baby and their babies might never know that they had been given up for adoption as society and circumstances had prevented the mothers from keeping them, even though their mother had loved them. There was nothing I could do other than to give the baby away, however sad it would be.

Millie and I had become good friends and one day she had a young man visit her. His name was Colin. Colin was a simple friendly man from a small village in Cornwall. He was very naïve and not used to the hectic city life of London and he longed to go back home but there was no work for him in Cornwall. He worked as a guard for the railway and did shift work, so it was only a few times a week that he was able to visit her. I told Millie that I had once had a boyfriend from Cornwall who also had worked on the railway, but Millie insisted Colin was not her boyfriend; he was just someone she knew. It was obvious to everyone but Millie that Colin had feelings for her. We were all surprised that Matron let Colin visit. One day he brought in a record player and, to impress Millie, he bought her 78rpm records to listen to. We played them very quietly in case we got told off, but Matron seemed to turn a blind eye and did not say a word about us playing the records. We girls would enjoy listening to all the rock and roll music and cry when Elvis Presley sung 'Heart Break Hotel' as we considered this home we were in was a heart-breaking place. Sometimes Millie and I would try to jive to 'Rock around the Clock' and the girls would laugh and giggle as we twisted around with our big tummies under our smocks, Millie in a pink-and-white polka dot and I in my red flowery one must have looked a sight, but we all laughed as we danced to the beat of the music. It was a relief to let our hair down and be able to enjoy ourselves after so many months of heartache. In a way we girls were living in a little cocoon in the 'home' and protected, to some extent, from a disapproving world. Matron came in one evening when she heard too much noise going on and said we had to go to bed at once as she did not want us all to go into labour at the same time. She said she did not mind us listening to music but we were not to jig around.

September gave way to October and the nights were drawing in. Some mornings it was foggy and my hands and feet froze when doing the washing in the outhouse. Sometimes I struggled to hang the washing on the line when there was a strong wind that sent the leaves and debris blowing like a hurricane around my legs, almost knocking me off of my feet. I was always so exhausted and uncomfortable; my back ached and my ankles were swollen, not that I could see them very well over my enormous 'bump'. To make matters worse, I also had a rash on my inner thighs where my legs had rubbed together, which prevented me from walking straight. The Sister had given me Robin's powdered starch to put on the rash, so one way and another I was not feeling good. One morning I was finishing off the Blue Room by swinging the bumper back and forth to give the floor a shine, when I suddenly felt unwell. My side hurt and my face was red and hot. Millie came in and told me to sit down for a while and she would help me finish off. That afternoon we went to antenatal and the doctor said my blood pressure was very high and I was to rest for the next couple of days. He said he wanted to see me the following Monday, then, if it was still too high, I would have to be admitted, so I must come prepared. I told Matron when I got back from the hospital and she said I could do light duties – cleaning the bathrooms and bedside cabinets.

On Sunday Millie washed and polished the Blue Room floor and in the afternoon she began to get contractions and she was sent by ambulance to the hospital. She had a baby boy the next day.

That same Monday I went to the hospital alone; the doctor examined me and said that, as my blood pressure was still too high, I was to be admitted. As I followed a nurse along a corridor, there was a side room and I saw a nurse putting silver instruments into a sterilizer. The room was piled high with silver metal bedpans, kidney-shaped dishes, and what I thought were prongs of all sizes. It really unnerved me as I did not have a clue what they were for and they looked like instruments of torture to me. I was shown to a bed in a very long ward. I tried to see if I could see Millie but she must have been in another ward. The curtains were pulled around the bed and I was asked to undress and put on a white gown. When the nurse returned she had a tray with water, shaving brush and soap at the ready. I had not been prepared for the humiliation of being shaved down below. I gritted my teeth in embarrassment. I was then given an awful oily substance to drink and taken to theatre and strung up like a chicken. The doctor said to a nurse that I did not have much water and that it might be a problem. By this time I was ready to freak out and cried out that I wanted to go home; I wanted my mum. But my cries fell on deaf ears. I was taken back to the ward and just when I thought I couldn't take much more I was given an enema with what felt like a bucket of hot soapy water. On top of all this, I was as sick as a dog. That evening I started to get pains in my lower back.

It was two long days later, on Wednesday, 17 October 1956, at 3.15 p.m., I had my baby with the help of forceps and gas and air. I had lots of stitches inside and out. Exhausted and weak, I marvelled at the beautiful baby boy I held in my arms. I was not allowed out of the bed for seven days, which made me feel trapped and vulnerable. I hated visiting time when husbands and family gathered around to see their new additions. No one came to visit me or marvel at my lovely baby son, so I would put my head under the sheet and pretended to be asleep until visiting time was over. One of the nurses was very offhand to me when she was taking my stitches out. I said 'ouch' as she nipped me and she snapped at me, saying it was my own fault that I was in hospital. I cried so much that I could hardly catch my breath. Later I complained to the hospital matron when she was on her visits around the wards, 'Why do people have to be so unkind and judgemental about situations they know nothing about?' The hospital matron just smiled and nodded her head and moved to the next patient as if I had not said a word. I stayed in hospital for a further seven days. The second week I was shown how to bath my baby. I had difficulty with breastfeeding; it was so painful for me that I was made to put these awful glass things on my nipples to encourage them to enlarge, but it did no good, so my baby was bottle-fed. I knew it did not matter very much as when I returned to the 'home' I would be bottle-feeding anyway, in preparation for the baby to go to its adoptive parents.

After two weeks a Sister came to meet me and the baby and we returned to the mother and baby home.

Chapter 26

I followed Sister Freda into the nursery; I wondered why she was the only sister that wore a green uniform instead of a grey one like the other sisters. She had an air of authority about her.

'Come in,' she said, walking briskly ahead of me and taking a peep at the sleeping babies as she passed the little cream-coloured cribs, 'and I will show you where to put your baby.'

It felt strange going into the nursery; it was only the staff and mothers that were ever allowed to enter there and, although I had heard the babies crying, I had never actually been into this place that smelt of cleanliness and soap and talcum powder. The room was very large, light and airy and had big windows, almost from floor to ceiling, with pale-green curtains hanging from metal rails. There were ten cotton-covered cribs standing side by side along one edge of the room. On top of a long white-painted unit there was a pile of terry towelling nappies next to a set of scales, and also a number of layette baskets filled with baby talcum powder, cotton wool, safety pins and baby soap. Sister pointed to the large sterilizing unit filled with baby bottles and teats; she said mothers were only to breastfeed for about two weeks before the babies would be bottle-fed. I explained that I was bottle-feeding Martin already. 'Oh well,' she said, 'not to worry. Lots of mums can only bottle-feed.' On the floor beside the unit were a few white-lidded enamel buckets stacked inside one another and about nine or ten cream-coloured baby's plastic baths.

I gently laid Martin, who was fast asleep, into the cot. At one time I use to think all babies looked the same, but after giving my baby a gentle kiss, I quickly took a peek at the other sleeping babies and decided these babies, although sweet, were not anywhere near as lovely as my little one. I was so proud of him; I considered he was the most beautiful baby ever to have been born. He had lots of dark hair and big eyes and when he looked at me, I just knew he recognized me as his mum.

'Come on, Rose,' said the Sister, shooing me out. 'You can't stay in here. Out you go, and you can come back at feed time. Now you must go and rest, on your tummy, with a pillow beneath it to help to get your figure back.'

I disliked leaving my baby in the nursery; he had always been beside me in the hospital. I reluctantly went up the stairs to the Blue Room where other girls were quietly resting. I had forgotten how quiet the house was in the afternoons and did not want to disturb them, so I pulled the pillow down the bed and laid on my stomach. My mind raced, and a cold fear and panic went through my body. How on earth was I going to cope with giving Martin away if I didn't even want to leave him for such a short while in the nursery? I tried to shake off the trembling inside of me. Now I understood how the girls must have felt when they had to leave their babies for good. I told myself I had to only think about each day as it came and enjoy the little time we have together; I had to do the only thing I could do and that was to give my baby to someone else to care for.

At feed time Millie showed me her baby boy. 'Isn't he lovely?' she said. 'I have named him Samuel – Sam for short.'

Jean and Helga showed me their babies, too, which they

169

had had two days after me. 'My baby's name is Peter, after my father who died a year ago,' said Jean.

Helga said her baby's name was Winston. 'As he will grow up to be a famous film star, Winston is a good strong name to have.' Helga had dreams of being a famous film star herself and she had had acting and dancing lessons before she had become pregnant by a sleazy married photographer. Helga wanted to be like her mother, who was an actress and model. Helga adored her, even though her mother had not bothered to visit or to get in touch since she had brought her here.

I held my baby in my arms to proudly show them. 'My beautiful baby boy is named Martin Paul, and no,' I said, smiling, 'it is not after anyone or because I want him to be famous, but just because I like the name.' I snuggled him to me; I loved the smell of the baby powder and the softness of his skin. 'Besides he looks as if he should be named Martin; it suits him.'

'It doesn't matter what you name them,' said Anna, a girl from the Yellow Room, who was feeding her baby girl. 'When they are adopted,' she added sadly, 'the new parents will change their names so it really doesn't matter at all.' The girl looked as if she was going to cry as this was her last day with her baby. This took the joy out of showing our babies off for a few minutes before I said, 'Well, up until then my baby is Martin Paul.'

I had noticed that the little girl Averill's bed had been empty and had assumed she was in hospital after having her baby. 'What did Averill have – a boy or girl? And when will she be back?' I asked Millie.

Millie replied, 'She had a little boy last week but the nursery Sister said she won't be returning as the baby was taken from her immediately after she had it. I don't know why, though.'

'Oh I hope everything turns out all right for her.'

I learnt later, from the nursery sister, that sometimes the

adoptive parents had not been approved or there were delays, so some of the babies went into children's homes before being placed. 'But this doesn't mean there won't be people ready for your babies,' she reassured us. This upset me; if Martin went into a children's home first, before being given away, it would be so unsettling for him. This also explained to me why sometimes a woman by herself would turn up to take the babies; it must have been the social workers taking them to the children's homes.

The more I was with Martin the more I thought that I would not be able to cope with him going away. In the evening, when the lights were out, I expressed my feelings to the other girls in a low whisper and we racked our brains for some way to keep our babies.

'I am going to ask my aunt if I can live with her again,' said Millie. 'She can only say no. If not, Samuel will have to be adopted; I have no option.' Millie's mother had died young and her father had remarried and had no place for Millie in his new life. She had lived with her aunt and Millie said she had treated her aunt very badly by running wild and staying out all night and not doing a thing she was told. Her aunt was unable to cope with her and then when Millie became pregnant her aunt told her to leave, so she was unsure whether her aunt would have her back after behaving in such a bad way.

'I don't suppose she will have me back but I can only ask.'

'We could get a live-in housekeeper's job,' said Jean.

'How do you go about that then?' Helga and I asked.

'Don't know,' said Jean. 'But I know these jobs do exist.'

A few weeks later, when Martin was five weeks old, I was in the nursery just after the 2 p.m. feed when Matron came in and said that I had a visitor. My heart began to race as I rose to put Martin back into the cot. Was it the social worker here to tell me that Martin was ready to go? Please, God, not yet. Please let me have him for a little longer.

'No, Rose, don't put him down,' said Matron. 'Bring your baby with you. You can go into the other room with him.' I was now very worried indeed as no one took babies out of the nursery and into the dining room; it was forbidden to do so. I cuddled Martin even closer to me. Matron opened the door to the room and I hesitated before I slowly entered. I was shocked and surprised to see my mother standing there; I could hardly believe it.

There was no embracing, just a polite 'Hello' to each other.

'Well, aren't you going to let me hold my grandson then?' Mum said, breaking the ice and taking him out of my arms.

I was so overwhelmed I could not speak for a while.

'My! He is so small and what a lot of hair he has.' Mum rocked him in her arms. I mumbled for her to sit down in case she dropped him. 'Of course I won't drop him! I have had enough babies, haven't I?'

I didn't know what to say to Mum but it was good to see her admiring her grandson.

'He's lovely,' she said, rocking him. 'He looks just like John.'

'Yes, I know he does, Mum.' Martin did look like John, but I did not even want to think about him; he was out of my life for good.

'I hear you have named him Martin. You should have called him John, seeing he looks so much like him.' Martin gave Mum a little smile; I didn't know if it was just wind or if it was a genuine smile, but Mum was thrilled.

'He is lovely,' she repeated. 'Look, he smiled at me again.' Mum tickled him under the chin. 'Who is a gorgeous boy then?'

'Yes Mum, I know he is lovely,' I said sadly, 'but unfortunately he is going to have a new family soon. He will have a new mum and dad and new grandparents, too.'

Mum carried on making cooing noises to the baby before answering seriously: 'Is that what you want, Rose?'

'No, of course not, Mum, but what choice have I got? I love him so much and if there was a way I could keep him I would.'

Mum gently handed Martin to me and I took him back into the nursery.

'Don't worry too much,' she said when I returned. 'He will be well cared for by his new parents. They may even be rich and he could have all the things you never had.' Mum tried to look as if she believed what she was saying, but I could tell she was unhappy. I was filled with remorse for having caused so much worry for her and my dad.

'Martin may go into a children's home first and that would be awful, Mum,' I said.

'Well, there is nothing you can do about it,' Mum said sharply. 'You can't come home, especially with a baby. What would the neighbours say and how could Dad and I face everybody, especially Mrs Baggers. Can you imagine? It would be all over the neighbourhood in no time. Your dad doesn't want you to come home, but I may be able to persuade him to let you come home without the baby. I will try to talk to him.'

I put my head down. 'Yes, you're right I know, but, Mum, I love him so much – it's going to be so difficult to part with him.' I was on the brink of crying again.

Mum stood to leave. She looked as choked up as me when she said goodbye. She kissed me on the cheek before hurrying out the door. After she went I put my hand to my cheek. I couldn't remember a time when Mum had kissed me before. I felt numb and that old, dark, deep painful feeling returned in the pit of my stomach. What is going to happen to me when I have to part with my baby and leave here? I missed my mum, my brothers and Sister Joyce and also little Joan, who was still in hospital. Where would I and Martin be in a year's time, I wondered, or five years' time? Would Martin know when he grew up how I loved him and wanted to keep him? I only wished I knew.

A week later Millie had a letter from her aunt and she joyfully told us she was leaving the following day to live with her; her aunt said she could also take the baby to live with her as well. Millie was overjoyed and we all were so pleased for her. I missed Millie when she left. She said she would write often to me.

We had a visit from the vicar at the end of November. He took the evening service in the chapel and we girls were lectured by him on the sinful acts we had committed. He said we were to come to the front and kneel down before him and beg for God's forgiveness. We went, one by one, to the front and knelt and, with our heads bent low, we did ask God for his forgiveness. We did believe we were sinful and had committed a dreadful crime and needed forgiveness. We would have been frowned upon by Matron and the Sisters if we hadn't co-operated. After this lecture the vicar said we were going to perform a Christmas nativity play and he would be returning to watch this just before Christmas and all of us were to take part. This really annoyed me and I grumbled to the other girls later: 'Blinking nerve he has. He's got a bloody cheek treating us as school kids. I am sixteen years old and a mother for goodness' sake. Who the heck does he think he is?'

But every evening from then on was spent rehearsing the nativity play. I suppose, for a short while, this took our minds off of our problems. I was given the part of one of the Three Kings and had to sing 'Myrrh is mine, its bitter perfume breathes a life of gathering gloom.' Yeah, right! I thought, that just about sums it up for me, nothing but gloom ahead, a life without my baby, my precious lovely boy.

As it happened, I never did get to play the part in the nativity play.

Chapter 27

It was a wet windy winter's day when I returned to the 'Home' from the hospital after being there for my postnatal examination. I kicked off the brown fallen leaves that had stuck to the heel of my shoes and rang the doorbell. Sister Ann opened the front door, and I quickly went inside. I shook the rain from my hair and took my sopping-wet coat off and rushed towards the stairs. I intended to change out of my wet things as soon as I could do so and then to wash out the memory of the postnatal examination by washing my hair. 'Just a moment, Rose,' said Sister Ann. 'Matron wants to see you in her office in about five or ten minutes' time.'

My heart skipped a beat. It could only be trouble if Matron wanted to see me. I hurried up the stairs into the Blue Room and hung my coat over the radiator to dry and sat on the bed for a few minutes, drying my hair with a towel. Blast, I thought, I will have to wait now until later to wash my hair. I was cold and my heart was now pounding. Take deep breaths, I thought, trying to calm my nerves. I breathed in, out, in, out. I tried to reassure myself; it may not mean trouble just because she wants to see me.

I tapped lightly on the door and heard her voice say, 'Come in!'

I paused, summoning up the courage to go in.

Matron was sitting behind her desk. She held a blue fountain pen, and an open folder lay on the green blotting pad. 'Take a seat, Rose.' I gingerly sat down. 'How did you get on at the hospital today?'

'Everything was all right, Matron.' I studied her well-scrubbed face for any sign of what was to come, but was unable to read her deadpan expression or to see what was behind the beady eyes behind her owl glasses.

'As you know, Rose, it is some weeks since you had your baby and I want to now discuss with you what is going to happen about the adoption of your baby and where you will be going to when you leave here.'

I tugged at my woollen sleeve and pulled a blue thread out, then tried to tuck it back in again.

Matron noticed how nervous I was, but said nothing to put me at ease; she carried on in a low monotonous voice. 'In the next couple of weeks your baby will be going into a children's home until he can be placed with his adoptive parents. You will then have three months before you sign the final adoption papers. Now about you – do you think you will be able to return to your parents' home?'

My voice was shaky. 'I don't know, Matron. My mother said she would ask my father but I haven't heard from her.'

'In that case, then, I will write to your parents to ask if you can return to live with them. If not, we will have to make other arrangements for you; for instance, you can go into a hostel for young homeless people. That's all I have to say to you today. I will also be in touch with the social worker to keep her informed of what is going to happen about the baby. I have nothing more to say, so you may now go.'

With that I was dismissed and she returned to her paperwork. It was as if now I had had the baby no one cared what would happen to me; I would be just cast aside like an unwanted peanut shell. I hurried back to the Blue Room and threw myself onto the bed and burst into tears. I knew this day would come but I still seemed unprepared for it. I would have to part with my baby son and I loved him so much. God help me, I cried; I don't want to let him go. After I had calmed down I splashed my red, puffy face in the bathroom. Anger was rising in me. How dare they steal my baby just because I had nowhere to go. I studied myself in the old, flaking chipped mirror on the wall and said aloud, 'Enough is enough: I will not be a victim anymore.' I seemed to gain an inner strength and returned to Matron's office. My heart was pounding.

I heard her voice say, 'Come in!' She lifted her eyebrows in surprise at seeing me. 'Have you forgotten something?'

'Yes,' I said defiantly, standing in front of her desk. 'I forgot to tell you that Martin will not be going into a children's home and he will not be going for adoption either. I am going to keep him. He is mine and I will not part with him.'

Matron cocked an eyebrow. 'Sit down, Rose,' she said sharply. 'You are obviously very upset at this news about what will happen, but you knew this time would come when your baby would be leaving you.'

'I don't want to sit down. I have already told you I am not going to give my baby up.'

'Sit down, Rose,' Matron demanded. I did not move. She took a deep breath and thought for a moment. Her cold eyes were steely grey behind her black-framed glasses and I noticed she had whitish, cloudy circles around her pupils. She gave a half-insincere smile and then threatened through gritted teeth: 'Sit down, I said.'

I did as I was told.

'Now let me tell you a few home truths,' she said 'Firstly, you have nowhere to live. Secondly, you will not be able to support a child, and thirdly, to keep your baby is a very selfish act indeed. Not only will people call you names, but also your baby will be called names when he goes to school as he has no father. Is this what you want? Go on tell me, is

177

that what you want?' She did not wait for an answer. 'Adoptive parents can give him so much more than you ever can. Now go to your room and we will not say any more about this matter.'

I left the room feeling rejected. It was pointless trying to convince the Matron that I was serious about keeping my baby, I knew in my heart now that, no matter what happened, I would not be giving Martin up. I would fight tooth and nail for him. He was mine and no one else was going to have him. There just had to be a way. I prayed silently: 'Please let me keep him, God, please, please; he belongs with me, his mother.'

I was sullen for days and did not want to mix very much with the other girls, but I cheered up a little when I received a letter from Millie. She wrote that she had married Colin, and as he worked for the railway they had applied for the accommodation allocated for rail workers. In the meantime they had moved to a furnished flat in Fulham. I was very pleased for her. I knew she did not love Colin but she had found a way to be a family. I told the other girls about Millie and they were all pleased for her as well. Helga said she wished she could meet someone to marry her and keep her baby. Jean said she could not marry someone she did not love no matter what, but understood the reasons why Millie had married Colin.

One morning, when I was still feeling very down, I had given Martin a bath and I was shaking the Johnson's baby powder onto his soft skin when Sister Freda told me off for putting too much on. I retaliated and snapped at her saying, 'I bought the powder and Martin is my baby and I will put on however much I please, so mind your own business and shut up!' Sister Freda turned on her heels and stormed out. I knew she would be going straight to Matron's office.

Later that morning, when we had finished doing our chores, a few of us girls were just on our way down the stairs when I was confronted by Sister Francis. 'Rose Handleigh, I hear you have been extremely rude to Sister Freda,' she said abruptly, blocking my way on the stairs. The girls carried on down.

'No I did not,' I replied. 'I just told her the truth that the powder was mine, so therefore I could use as much as I wanted to.'

'You are a rude, nasty girl. I will report you to Matron.' She gave me a hard shove on my shoulder. I almost fell backwards down the stairs. To stop myself falling, I shoved her back with one hand and grabbed the handrail with the other. I don't know who was more shocked, me or her. Sister Francis and I stared defiantly at each other. All my frustrations were rising in me. The other girls stood with gaping mouths at the bottom of the stairs. Jean broke the ice by running back up the stairs. 'Don't, Rose, don't do anything you will regret; just leave it,' she said loudly, pulling me away from the Sister.

I ran down the stairs with Jean still tugging at my arm. In the dining room the girls who had seen what had happened soon told the other girls about it. I sat sideways on a dining chair, my heart going nineteen to the dozen. 'Oh my God, what have I done? What will Matron do? She'll most probably chuck me out without my baby.'

'Don't worry, Rose, we saw everything. We will say that the Sister pushed you first and you only tried to stop yourself from falling,' said Helga. The girls all agreed that this is what happened and said they would back me up.

'Thank you, but don't do that – you will only get yourselves into trouble, too.'

At lunchtime, we all waited for the bomb to drop, but nothing happened. I ate in silence aware that the Sisters as well as the girls were watching me.

'Perhaps nothing will happen. Perhaps Sister Freda and Sister Francis have not said anything to Matron,' whispered Helga later.

'Don't be daft!' said Jean. 'Of course they would have said something. They are just making their minds up what to do next.'

This did not make me feel any better and at bedtime I was restless and could hardly sleep with worry. The suspense was awful and my mind was doing overtime as to what would happen next.

After breakfast next day, I was finally called into the Matron's office.

'I have been in touch with the social worker and reported your bad behaviour towards Sister Freda and Sister Francis. Your bad behaviour will not be tolerated in this house; you have overstepped the mark. Your social worker has been to see your mother and asked if you could return home today. As yet I have not heard whether you can or not, but whatever happens your baby will be going into care today. You, Rose, will be leaving here today with the social worker, so go and pack your things now.'

With that I was dismissed. A shiver went down my spine. I could not speak or cry but could only stand for a moment before turning and leaving the room. As I went, I was conscious of her eyes boring into my back.

I went silently to the blue room and packed my few belongings into my old case. I took the baby clothes from the locker and stuffed them into a brown paper carrier bag. The packets of baby nappies I piled onto the bed then sat beside them thinking about everything that had happened. Would I be going into a homeless hostel? Would I just be thrown out of the door? Where would Martin go? Should I just run away with him? No, I couldn't do that. I couldn't walk the streets – it wouldn't be fair – and they would soon find us and take him from me anyway.

Helga and Jean burst into the room. 'What's happening? What are they going to do?'

'I don't know what is going to happen other than that

Martin will be taken from me today and I will be thrown out of the door, possibly to walk the streets like my nan does,' I replied in a slow calm voice, swallowing back the tears.

Helga and Jean sat either side of me and tried to comfort me by wrapping their arms around my shoulders.

'Wherever you go, Rose, you will let us know, won't you? We will miss you like mad.' I knew they had a lot to cope with and they were concerned about the day coming soon when they would be parting with their babies, so I just nodded 'yes'. I did not want them worrying about me.

After afternoon tea I heard a ring on the doorbell. I peeped out of the dining-room window; it was the social worker. I did not know what to do; I panicked as my whole insides seemed to go into a spin. I began to tremble and felt sick.

'What can I do?' I whispered to Jean. 'I'm scared, Jean.'

Jean bit on her bottom lip. There was nothing she could say. She put her arm around me.

A Sister poked her head around the door. 'Rose, you are wanted.'

I walked slowly out of the door as if I was a condemned criminal going to the gallows. I went into the Matron's office and was given a lecture by the social worker on bad behaviour before I was told to fetch my things as I had to leave.

I began to cry and burst out, 'I want to say goodbye to Martin first and I also want you to know that I am not parting with him because I want to but because I love him and want him to know this someday and also that he was stolen from me by you all.'

They did not reply as I turned and left to go into the nursery. I picked up my baby and sat down to cuddle him for the last time. 'I love you little one,' I said as I took his tiny hand in mine. He gave a little smile. 'You remember this when you grow up. You had a mummy that loved you very much.' I put Martin down and left the room quickly before I broke down again, as I did not want him to see me cry as it might have disturbed him, as babies can sense distress. As I left the nursery I was surprised to see my mother storming through the front door.

'Mum!' I cried, running towards her. 'They are going to take my baby away.'

'We'll see about that,' Mum said firmly.

'Mrs Handleigh, I must ask you to wait in the dining room and not cause a scene. It will upset the other girls,' said Matron.

Mum ignored her and said to me, 'Rose, go fetch your belongings. We are leaving right now. You and your baby are coming home with me.'

'But, Mum, what about Dad and what about the neighbours?'

'We will face them together. Now are you coming or not?'

I ran up the stairs as fast as I could and struggled down with mine and Martin's things. There were heated words going on between my mother, Matron, the social worker and the Sisters.

'Mrs Handleigh, I will not allow you to come in here like this and cause such a disturbance,' said Matron.

The social worker said, 'Mrs Handleigh, you have not thought this through.'

'Rules are rules and a place has been found for Rose's baby so you must leave right now.'

'Sod you and your bloody petty rules. I am taking my daughter and grandson home right now, so stick your rules. You are not taking my daughter or my grandson anywhere, so there. Stick your rules where ever you like, up your backside if necessary.' Mum looked a scary sight when she was angry. 'Come on, Rose, go and get your baby – we're off.'

I gave the bags to Mum to hold on to and hurried to the nursery door. Matron blocked my way. 'Rose, this is ridiculous. You and your mother have not thought this through enough,' she said, trying to gain some authority over the situation. She stood firm and would not let me enter.

'Move!' I spat. But she did not budge. My face twisted in anger, my eyes blazing; we were standing nose to nose. 'I said MOOOOVE!' I repeated through gritted teeth.

She winced as if I was going to strike her, and she moved quickly to one side. I rushed past her into the nursery and hurriedly took Martin from his cot and wrapped him in a blanket. He was asleep and gave a little stretch as I picked him up and I gave him a little kiss. 'Come on, baby. We are going home.'

I grabbed a made up bottle of milk and rushed back to the hallway.

The sisters, Matron and the social worker did nothing to stop us leaving; shocked, they just stood there with open mouths.

Mum held Martin and I trotted behind her with the bags. I took one last look back as we walked up the gravel driveway and I saw Helga and Jean, with tears in their eyes, waving and smiling at me from the window.